TRADITIONAL HMONG
MARRIAGE CEREMONY
VALUES

Choua Mouavangsou

Traditional Hmong Marriage Ceremony Values

by Choua Mouavangsou

Copyright ©2010 by Choua Mouavangsou, PsyD., MFT.

Cover Image: Traditional Hmong Marriage Umbrella

ISBN: 1-55605-400-9

978-155605-400-6

Library of Congress Control Number:2009943624

Wyndham Hall Press
5050 Kerr Rd
Lima, OH 45806
www.wyndhamhallpress.com

Printed In The United States of America

DEDICATION

To my parents, Xay Leng Mouavangsou and Ka Xiong Mouavangsou, for instilling your wisdom and knowledge upon me without reservations and for continuously inspiring me and having high expectations of all my endeavors. Your constant encouragement, support, friendship and above all gentle love have always been present and felt throughout my life journey.

Also, to my children, for you are the bearer, preserver, and champion of our way of life, our traditions, our cultures and the very essence of what is truly liked being a Hmong. May you, your children and your children's children continue to value and practice Hmong's unique rituals and customs.

ACKNOWLEDGMENTS

I am greatly indebted to the many wonderful people who have been an integral part of my life journey and contributed greatly to the development and completion of this book. Additionally, they have inspired me to dream and rise to the occasion of change.

My most grateful appreciation and heartfelt love goes to my husband, Zongkai (Kua) Vang, for taking this journey with me and being the rock and calm water for both of us, especially during the winds of adversity and turbulence. I thank Zongkai so much for embracing my aspirations and having patience and understandings as I strive to achieve them. He was the wind beneath my wings and the optimizer who supported and encouraged me throughout this challenging endeavor. I accredit a great deal of this book to him, as he tirelessly provided me with constructive feedbacks on the multiple drafts of the manuscript and ensured that careful attention was given to all minute details.

I would like to express a most sincere and grateful acknowledgement and thanks to my father, Xay Leng Mouavangsou, for sharing his gifts of traditional Hmong marriage rituals with me so that accurate and relevant information could be referenced throughout this book. My father's wisdom and value of human interconnection and personal humbleness toward individualistic histories are magnitudinal gifts, which allowed him to have friendships from far and wide. I wish that he could have lived to witness the realization of his hopes and dreams, especially, with the publication of this book.

I wanted to express a great deal of gratitude to my mother, Ka X. Mouavangsou, for spending precious moments with me in sharing her talents and gifts of being a shaman, herbalist, diagnostician, and in using pure magic "khawv koob". Her contribution on shamanism and the art of traditional healings were extremely resourceful for this project. I thank my lucky stars and wonderful blessings for this very gifted, walking-Hmong-dictionary, and extremely wise person with a keen mind and high intellect as my mom, personal confidant, mentor, and reference guide throughout this lengthy project.

Throughout the endeavors that I have undertaken, I could not have done them without two humble individuals whose understandings and patience I could never have done without, my mother-in-law and father-in-law, May Yang Vang and Xia Shua Vang. I wanted to thank you them for their support and encouragement from the very beginning of this journey. There were many traditional events and family functions that they have forgiven me for not participating due to my times spent on this project.

My uncle Bla Neng Vang was very resourceful with his knowledge on traditional rituals and Hmong's way of life. I thank him for spending long hours tirelessly sharing his expertise on Hmong traditional marriage ceremony rituals so that the information provided would be accurate.

A sincere acknowledgement and appreciation to my personal counselor, esteemed professor, project chair, and friend, Dr. Toni Knott for unselfishly sharing her knowledge and wisdom and spending endless hours reviewing and guiding this project. Her gracious feedback and inputs have made this study more meaningful and relevant to the Hmong and the profession of Organization Development. Her dedication, compassion, understanding, and leadership brought this project to the forefront to completion.

A number of professors and mentors have contributed their invaluable time and feedback to this book and many times have read the many drafts of this manuscript more than once in its entirety.   I would like to extend a sincere acknowledgement and gratitude to Dr. Carl Mack, Dr. Karen Erickson, Dr. Larry B. Anders, Dr. Sherry Camden-Anders, and Dr. Juan C. Garcia for their encouragement and support.

This book would not have existed without the vision and inspiration of Mary Jane Cavanaugh. She saw the importance and possibilities of this book during its early stages and suggested putting it into print. My life journey will be forever changed because of this individual. I owe a great deal of gratitude to Mary Jane and would especially like to recognize her.

Last but certainly not least, I would like to express my most sincere acknowledgement, thanks, and with the highest of gratitude to the individuals who have shared their stories, journeys and experiences so that I can bring life to the richness of our traditional practices and way of life. I am greatly indebted to you for graciously agreeing to be interviewed and sharing your thoughts and experiences for this study. Without you, this project would not have existed. Thank you so much for your time, honesty, and contribution to this study.

ABSTRACT

Through the evolution of time, people often migrated to various regions to survive. Over the centuries, the Hmong are among those ancient people who have migrated from one location to another in search of the peace and freedom to live and practice their traditional way of life in solidarity. As they migrated into the various regions, they often had to live within the cultures of those new environments while striving to maintain their traditional rituals and practices. As one of many refugee groups migrating to the United States, the Hmong have made radical changes to their traditional practices, particularly traditional Hmong marriage ceremony rituals.

A qualitative study using semi-structured, face-to-face and telephone interviews was conducted to discover factors that have affected change to the traditional Hmong marriage ceremony among the 0.5-generation Hmong participants. The 0.5-generation Hmong are individuals who were born in Laos and raised and educated in the United States with a common knowledge of both Hmong and American cultures. All of the participants in this study resided in the states of California and Utah in the United States.

Thematic analysis was the methodology approach used for analyzing the qualitative data in this study. The data were themed and conclusions were drawn based on the participants' interview responses. Some of the themes identified by the participants regarding the factors that have resulted in changes to the traditional Hmong marriage ceremony rituals were (a) time required for marriage rituals, (b) lack of knowledge of the rituals, (c) religion, (d) significance of Hmong rituals, (e) assimilation and acculturation to the American culture, (f) education, (g) mixed race marriages, (h) money required for rituals, (i) language, and (j) the shift in thinking from collectivism to individualism. These factors have influenced some of the Hmong to consider different and varied marriage ceremony approaches upon marrying in the United States.

Although these participants have married within the traditional Hmong marriage arrangement ceremonies, they were open to their children's preferences and choice of marriage arrangement options. The essential marriage elements were continued to be practiced by the 0.5-generation Hmong even though modifications have been made to some of the traditional Hmong marriage ceremony rituals. With the Hmong quickly adapting to and adopting the American culture, there were high expectations that the Hmong will continue to preserve and practice their traditional marriage practices and rituals with their marriage ceremony preferences.

TABLE OF CONTENTS

"A journey of a thousand miles begins with a single step"
(Lao-Tzu, 2008).

To all of my children, we have made our final journey to America, the land of boundless opportunities. Knowledge and wisdom are not gender specific now but are for all those who thirst for them by seeking greater understanding and comprehension of their wonders.

Xay Leng Mouavangsou,
personal communication,
June 3, 1994

PROLOGUE

Preservation of history is to retain the past, as it applies to the present and future of a group of people. I have always been fascinated by the past and intrigued by the present of the Hmong culture. With such heightened interest in the Hmong history and how the richness of the culture has been practiced and preserved over time, I have been collecting and documenting stories, rituals, chants, life experiences, and unique customs and traditions that are specific to being a Hmong ever since I was a young girl.

Although the culture of the Hmong is complex, with many rituals that are customarily passed on and performed by gender-specific individuals, I am honored and humbled that my father had allowed me the opportunity to document the rituals and observed traditions that are family specific as well as the customs that are applicable to being a Hmong ever since I could remember. Perhaps my curiosity gave me greater access to certain information and traditional activities than other females. When I was in my late teens, I had always managed to be in the front row watching rituals being performed and as I grew older my curiosity led me to ask more in-depth questions about them; that was when my father started to allow me to videotape and audiotape the ceremonies and rituals that were being performed. It was odd at the time, in the mid-1980s, that my father would allow me such a privilege as a female to be among males as a spectator and sometimes take part in some male-dominated rituals.

I recall distinctively the summer that he decided to share detailed information about traditional Hmong marriage ceremonies with me. It was a hot evening 12 years ago; our family sat around in the living room of my parents' home just having casual conversations about life and reminiscing about the journey for our family up to that point when my father, a prominent Hmong *mejkoob*, asked me to videotape him as he demonstrated the sequential rituals of the traditional Hmong marriage ceremonies. That evening, I recorded all that my father knew about traditional Hmong marriage ceremony rituals late into the night. As I recorded these rituals, my father explained each step of the rituals and discussed the significance of each ceremony in detail. I was fascinated and amazed at my father's ability to account for the detailed rituals and recite and sing the numerous marriage songs with such ease. Little did I know then that a pure-hearted inquisitiveness would turn out to be an excellent resource for my dissertation project later in my life.

My father and I often had lengthy conversations about life in America and forecast what the future would be like for his children and grandchildren. In our conversations, he stated that the younger Hmong generations in America were preoccupied with a fast-paced life and might not be able to learn the various Hmong rituals; therefore, he wanted me to preserve his knowledge of traditional rituals for his grandchildren and future generations to appreciate and use if they should choose to continue practicing the traditional Hmong arts and rituals. He further explained that knowledge and wisdom were not gender specific but rather for those who thirst for them by seeking greater understanding and comprehension of the wonders of a people through having a comprehensive knowledge of them. I was so lucky to have had the opportunity to capture my father's multiple talents and wisdom in the time that I had with him. It continues to amaze me how he could be so knowledgeable and retain so much information about the Hmong customs in one lifetime.

In addition to gaining a great deal of in-depth information from my father, I also obtained a substantial amount of information from my husband's Hmong clan, especially from my Uncle Bla Neng Vang. In such a so-called double standard society of the Hmong where gender roles clearly draw a division between who would be given access to certain rituals and information, I feel that I am among many Hmong women who have finally broken that fine line between the genders. My husband's clan and their elders willingly and unselfishly shared their knowledge and wisdom with me about traditional Hmong marriage ceremonies as well as clan-specific rituals and history without reservation. I feel that although my father and the elders who willingly shared with me about our traditional way of life were raised and had lived in a double standard society, their views were starting to change since they resided in the United States.

It is with great curiosity for an insightful and comprehensive understanding of being a Hmong and how their rituals have withstood over time despite the many migrations resulting in encounters and interactions with various social groups and cultures that have interested me in studying the dynamics and evolution of the traditional Hmong marriage ceremony utilizing the lens of organization development. I am hopeful that this study will illuminate and provide a multidimensional understanding and perhaps greater appreciation of the traditional Hmong marriage ceremony why, I believe, is uniquely one of the hearts of the traditional Hmong culture.

Chapter 1
INTRODUCTION

From the beginning of time, people have constantly migrated from one region to another in search of a better life. For some, relocation was necessary to prevent persecution and extinction. In migrating to new lands, Morgan (1997) indicated that people "must achieve an appropriate relation with that environment if they are to survive" (p. 39). Goodstein and Burke (1995) stated that the need to change stems from an "external pressure rather than an internal desire" to change, and this change may be due to "social conditions that create long-term change" to organizations (p. 7).

The Hmong are a group of people who have a long history of migration from the valleys and rivers of China to the misty mountains of Southeast Asia and then to Western resettlement countries in search of the "freedom and independence" to be a "free people" even though they have been coerced, manipulated, and pressured to change, as they have struggled to maintain their customs and traditional practices while adapting to some of those societies' cultures to maintain peace and harmony and survive (Hamilton-Merritt, 1993, p. 3).

Schein (2005) stated:

> The strength of a given culture or subculture will depend on several factors: a) the strength of the convictions of the original founders and subsequent leaders; b) the degree of stability of the membership and leadership over a period of time; and c) the number and intensity of learning crises that the group has survived. (p. 366)

Regardless of what region, country, or continent that the Hmong have migrated to, they have managed to maintain a part of their traditional culture. They have strong cultural resiliency to change and yet managed to adapt and adopt enough of what was present in the new cultures to survive. The Hmong have an "open system" where their cultural organization is permeable enough to the current environment as to allow them the flexibility and ability to dictate the amount of oscillation and change between their traditional culture and those of the current environments' cultures (Beckhard & Harris, 1977, p. 59).

Goodstein and Burke (1995) discussed the need to make modification and adjustments "implementing modest changes that improve the organization's performance yet do not fundamentally change the organization" (p. 9). The Hmong are making changes to their ancient marriage ceremony ritual practices to meet the needs of the younger Hmong generation in America, but not necessarily changing who they are as a people. Their ancient culture has been sustained over the centuries of their migration. Although they have made changes in their migration to exist, the Hmong's fundamental philosophy and core beliefs and values of life are still being maintained. The Hmong's long-held value of democracy in their lives is similar to that of the values in the United States as well as the values or organizational development (OD; Freeman, 1996; Hardy, 1992; Organization Development Network, 2001).

Although often similar in values, cultural practices are vastly different between the mainstream society and Hmong. To survive and thrive in this country, the Hmong have quickly adapted to the Western culture of the United States (U.S.). Warren Bennis (cited in Egan, 2002) indicated that an organization needs to change to respond and adapt to the new challenge. Similarly, Tannenbaum and Hanna (1985) discussed in the journal article, "Holding on, Letting Go, and Moving on: Understanding a Neglected Perspective on Change," about the need to change and adapt to survive and grow due to the rapidly changing environment. Newman and Nollen (1998) stated that "As environments change, firms also must change to realign themselves with the new conditions, and those that do change will perform better" (p. 45). They also indicated that an organization must change to prevent stagnation. Cummings and Worley (2005) agreed and discussed the dynamics of cultural change and how an individual organization's culture can shape the members' beliefs and actions.

The Hmong are quickly adapting to the United States culture and society to align with the demands and are striving to keep pace and progress forward as productive citizens. Newman and Nollen (1998) stated that "systems, resources, and capabilities that fit with the environment are more likely to survive than firms with structure and processes that do not fit with the environment" (p. 43). They also found that "in rapidly changing environments, we observe more change in the population of organizations because old organizational forms do not fit the new environment conditions. It implies quantum and fundamental change in the firm's core value . . . structures, and capabilities" (p. 45).

> These are a useful starting point for understanding how change takes place. Although different in form, many of these models agree on fundamental characteristics, the first of which is the breakdown of the existing system, followed by a period of confusion, followed by convergence around new core values or paradigm. (Newman & Nollen, 1998, p. 45)

By viewing the traditional Hmong marriage ceremony from this standpoint of an *institution*, the Hmong marriage ceremony and traditions now are being merged with the institution of the *American wedding* ceremony to form a more enriched and emerging institution. As institutions merge, modifications are made. The Hmong are changing traditional Hmong marriage ceremonies to reflect more Americanized wedding ceremonies to meet the desires and needs of the younger Hmong generation living in the U.S. As they change their traditional practices, they may only choose to retain the most essential rituals as they incorporate them into an Americanized wedding. Ken Benne (cited in Freeman, 1996), stated, "I think they need a chance to influence the other as the other is influencing them. That becomes a joint thing" (p. 339). Because they have been living in the U.S. for over 35 years, it is inevitable that the Hmong will be influenced by the culture of this country, especially in their traditional practices, as they continue to move forward striving to be successful. Morgan (1997) stated, "Successful organizations seem to share 'configurations' or 'patterns' of distinctive characteristics that are appropriate for dealing with their particular environment" (p. 55).

> Effective firms in rapidly changing industries . . . are structured more flexibly than firms in slowly changing industries. Organizational change from this perspective is a process of "fitting" the organization more rationally with its relevant competitive environment. High performance, therefore, is a function of the right fit between an organization and its environment. (Newman & Nollen, 1998, p. 45).

The Hmong's values in life and the fundamental philosophy that the U.S. was founded on are a perfect fit for ideal radical change to take place.

Although one of the essential fabrics of the Hmong culture is that of the marriage tradition, the environment that a culture dwells in also plays an integral part of shaping and reforming that tradition. Forsyth (2006) discussed the need to change in order to belong to social groups in an environment. To be successful and advance and progress in this country with a sense of belonging, the Hmong are beginning to change some of their traditional practices to reflect those of their new country of residence.

Statement of the Problem

The traditional Hmong marriage ceremony is viewed as an institution where individuals, their families, and clans interact from the moment the marriage negotiations start to take place. Marriage is more than just a bond between two people and their immediate families. Symonds (2004) stated that marriage between two people for the Hmong is a bridge between two clans, which connects and ties kinships.

> A Hmong marriage is far more than a union between two people; it is one of a series of unions between clans and lineages. Marriage not only facilitates new alliances and family networks but repairs old alliances through the resolution of past disagreements. (p. 40)

Cummings and Worley (2005) discussed strategic change and approaches to organization change through "mergers, acquisitions, alliance formation, and network development" (p. 12).

The Hmong traditional marriage ceremonial practice is one of the cornerstone rituals of their culture that provided for social interactions and allowed interconnectedness among the Hmong. It is a lengthy marriage celebration honoring the past, present, and future relationships within the Hmong community.

However, because the culture of this country is different from that of the traditional Hmong culture, some modifications and changes to traditional marriage ceremonies and rituals have been made. Schein (2005) stated that an organizational culture has an "overall arching culture along with subcultures that vary in strength and degree of congruence with the total organization culture" (p. 366). The cultural context of traditional Hmong marriage ceremony is a subculture of the Hmong culture. Within the traditional Hmong marriage ceremony, subculture is another layer of subcultures, which are individual Hmong marriage ceremony preferences and practices. Some of the Hmong only select essential rituals to be performed during the marriage negotiations. Others choose to have only Americanized wedding ceremonies, while some have abandoned Hmong traditional marriage ceremonies altogether. There are some Hmong couples who have multiple marriage ceremonies to meet the desires of today's society while also fulfilling their parents' request for a traditional marriage ceremony. These marriage ceremony practices are all deviations from the traditional Hmong marriage ceremony rituals of the past and appear to be recent outcomes of resettlement into another culture.

Purpose of the Study

There have been a number of studies that have been conducted relative to Hmong marriages in their new environments. Mua's (2002) study focused on the issues that were related to the Hmong being uprooted from their traditional system in Laos to the United States and the factors that have affected Hmong marriages. He discussed Hmong marriages through the lens of religious perspectives, in particular Christianity. Meredith and Rowe (1986a, 1986b) also conducted a study examining the impact of a new culture on the Hmong's attitudes about marriage. Specifically, they focused on marriage preparation, marriage roles, and divorce. Dana (1993) explored the roles of men and women as they related to courtship and marriage. Additionally, Moua (2003) examined the traditional Hmong kinship, marriage, and family systems in the United States. He provided some understanding of the changes related to these areas and how they have affected the Hmong as they migrated to the U.S. Furthermore, Kunstadter (2004) conducted a study examining the Hmong marriage patterns in Thailand and how they have changed due to relocation, comparing the changes of the Hmong in Thailand to those in the United States. Finally, Bertrais (1978) provided a detailed description of the Hmong marriage arrangements and ceremonies along with documenting and depicting the descriptive marriage rituals, songs, and sequential progression of entire marriage ritual processes.

Although these studies have addressed various aspects of the Hmong's traditional marriage ceremonies, focusing on changes that have occurred, only a limited number of these studies alluded to, or mentioned factors that have affected the Hmong to change their traditional marriage ceremony practices and rituals. The importance and purpose of this study was to discover the factors that are responsible for the Hmong in changing their deeply rooted traditional marriage ceremonies after their resettlement in the United States. Although it is relevant to obtain information from the various age groups related to this issue, the researcher chose to study the 0.5-generation Hmong. The 0.5-generation Hmong are the individuals who were born in Laos, but have been raised and educated in the United States. The targeted population is considered to be the bridge between the old and the new Hmong generations. These individuals have solid foundations and cultural understandings of the traditional Hmong, however are fluent in the culture and language of the United States. Because of having solid foundations in both cultures, they are the ones who are motivated to make changes within their traditional culture to accommodate the culture and society of the U.S.

As Cummings and Worley (2005) indicated, the "readiness for change" will motivate members of an organization to make changes (p. 155). The authors also indicated that the members of the organization have to "create a vision . . . and reason for change and describes the desired future state" (p. 155). The 0.5-generation Hmong are the group that are ready for change, as they seem to be the most comfortable in deciding what traditions and rituals should be retained and the ones that need to be changed or modified to align with the society in which they now reside. Through these individuals' visions on balancing the retention of the Hmong's cultures and traditions while also embracing the American culture, their responses on marriage and marriage patterns will help in understanding the direction of future generations' traditional practices while capturing the lingering richness of the older generations' way of life regarding marriage ceremonies. Beckhard and Harris (1977) stated that the process of making changes in complex organizations should consider the following:

> 1) Diagnosing the present condition, including the need for change; 2) setting goals and defining the new state or condition after the change; 3) defining the transition state between the present and the future;
>
> 4) Developing strategies and action plans for managing this transition; 5) evaluating the change effort;
>
> 6) Stabilizing the new condition and establishing a balance between stability and flexibility. (p. 16)

The 0.5-generation Hmong are a group of individuals who are most concerned about having a balance of the cultural practices and are most likely to be the ones who will incorporate transitional changes and implement processes in the Hmong community to prepare them for a radical cultural shift through "managing transition" from the current Hmong cultural state to the future state (Cummings & Worley, 2005, p. 156). Additionally, Cummings and Worley discussed the need to have resources "building a support system for change agents, developing new competencies and skills, and reinforcing the new behaviors needed to implement the changes" (p. 156). The 0.5-generation Hmong appear to have the tools, resources, and support systems among each other, the older Hmong generations, and younger Hmong generations to change and transition the current Hmong marriage ceremony rituals into a more streamlined marriage ceremony in the future that would include both the traditional Hmong marriage ceremony and the new marriage ceremony practices that are reflected in those of the United States culture.

Using the Word Hmong Instead of Mong

There are two distinct Hmong dialects spoken within the Hmong community in Laos called White Hmong and Green Hmong. Different dialects often include difference in clothing and oftentimes in rituals and practices. Although the dialects are different, they are easily understood by both groups. Because there are subtle differences between the Green Hmong and the White Hmong traditional practices, the researcher chose to focus on the traditional Hmong marriage ceremony rituals of the Green Hmong. The researcher also chose to use the Green Hmong dialect to depict the elements of the traditional Hmong marriage ceremony rituals that are included throughout this research study. Although the word, Hmong, is a White Hmong terminology and spelling for Hmong, the researcher chose to use it instead of the Green Hmong terminology and spelling, Mong, since the word, Hmong, has been used in most of the related literature and is widely recognized.

Summary

The Hmong have a long history of migrating from one region to another in search of freedom and independence in order to live in harmony and practice their traditional way of life. In their constant search for a better life, the Hmong have maintained their unique and sophisticated customs and traditions. Due to the lack of freedom to live in solidarity in China, the Hmong migrated to nearby Southeast Asian countries, such as Burma, Thailand, Vietnam, and Laos. Because of the Hmong's involvement in the Vietnam War, they were forced to flee Laos seeking refuge in Thailand during the mid-1970s. Beginning in 1976, thousands of Hmong were granted permission to live in resettlement countries, including the United States, Canada, Argentina, France, Canada, Australia, and Germany. As the Hmong began to acculturate and assimilate into the customs and cultures of these host countries, many of them have changed and modified their traditional customs and rituals, especially the traditional marriage ceremony rituals, to reflect the cultural practices of those countries. This research study was created to focus on the factors that were influencing those changes and the related effects on the Hmong society and their respective clans.

Chapter 2

LITERATURE REVIEW

The literature review in this chapter highlights the dynamics of the traditional Hmong marriage ceremony's ritual practices with respect to the cultural adaptations as a result of environmental influences of relocation and resettlement in the United States. This chapter is composed of five sections.

The first section provides an analysis of the Hmong culture, particularly the traditional Hmong marriage ceremony ritual, as an organization through the lens of organization development. The second section features a brief overview of the Hmong's culture and history and movements from China to Laos. The third section is a description of the traditional Hmong marriage ceremony ritual practices in Laos and the importance of marriage songs, symbolism of artifacts and elements, and proverbs. The fourth section is focused on analyzing the significance of the assimilation and acculturation into the U.S. relative to traditional marriage ceremony practices, and finally, the fifth section provides a summary of this chapter.

Change Models and Organization Development(OD) Theories

Organization development theories and change models are broad and transformational, as they could be used and applied in any organizational context beyond the corporate world into public institutions, religious affiliations, professional organizations, individual, and personal change. The versatility of OD theories and models of change is applicable in any organizational context since OD theories and models of change transcend cultures, races, and languages. The Hmong culture and subculture of marriage ceremony rituals are vehicles of contexts that allow for the articulation and application of OD theories and models of change. Through examining the Hmong's cultural changes, insights and understandings were discovered about their quantum radical change upon movement and resettlement in the United States.

The Hmong culture and subcultures have changed rapidly after having lived in the United States for the short time of 33 years, with the alignment of their cultural practices with those of the United States culture. Schein (1999) indicated that "Central to any organization improvement program is the creation of a situation in which learning and change can take place by individuals and/or groups" (p. 4). He further discussed corporate culture and the relevancy to organizational progress. The Hmong have a strong belief about the power of collectivism and group cohesiveness with receptiveness to individual creativity as a springboard to group advancement through individual achievements. It is the work of the individualistic Hmong who are driven to be competitive and progressive that has been manifested in community advancement.

Schein (1985) discussed the subcultures that are evident and revolve within the organizational culture. He stated that an organizational culture has an "overall arching culture along with subcultures that vary in strength and degree of congruence with the total organization culture" (p. 366). The cultural context of traditional Hmong marriage ceremony is a subculture of the overall Hmong culture. Within the traditional Hmong marriage ceremony subculture is another layer of subcultures, which are manifested in individual Hmong marriage ceremony preference and practices.

Viewing the Hmong culture from Martin's (2002) three lenses of integrated, differentiated, or fragmented perspectives, the Hmong culture and subcultures can be analyzed as an integration of his integrated and differentiated perspectives. The Hmong culture is then identified and viewed as integrated because there are certain beliefs, values, and practices that have continued to be practiced that clearly defined them as they strived to be successful within the boundaries, policies, resources, and means of their new environment. The Hmong appear to have an open system in their culture and the environment in which they reside, which is an ideal match for opportunities for development and growth (Beckhard & Harris, 1997; Lawrence & Lorsch, 1969).

By specifically focusing on the Hmong subcultures of traditional Hmong marriage ceremonies, they can be examined from Martin's (2002) differentiated perspective where there are some differences between the subcultures within the culture. By analyzing these subcultures from this perspective, it allows for the flexibilities of individualistic preferences and choices without imposing mandates for the overall culture. It is within the multidimensional oscillation of the open systems within the subcultures, the Hmong culture, and the mainstream culture that the Hmong have made some radical changes in the last 3 decades since migrating to the United States (Beckhard & Harris, 1977). Based on Lawrence and Lorsch's (1969) perspectives regarding organization growth, the Hmong subcultures appear to operate within the two open systems of the United States culture and the Hmong culture; however, if there are potential hazards on the horizon within the subcultures, they then resort to the overall culture to regroup before moving forward.

Schein (1985) discussed the levels of corporate culture, which have four vital elements at the different levels of awareness that included basic assumptions, values, norms, and artifacts. In the Hmong subculture of traditional marriage ceremonies, there are symbolisms, artifacts, songs, chants, negotiations, and a multitude of complex components that ultimately constitute a marriage. Although the Hmong culture tolerates personal preferences and choices, there tend to be certain artifacts that are representative of a marriage that could be determined by the parents of the marrying couple or the Hmong community as a whole. The most symbolic artifact in a Hmong marriage process is the present of the Marriage Umbrella. It signifies the ancient protocol of a marriage negotiation process taking place between the marrying couple, their families, and clans. Although the Hmong have adapted some of their new country of residence's marriage practices and religions, the majority of the Hmong still require the groom's marriage party to have the Marriage Umbrella throughout the marriage process. Another such artifact that has continued to play a vital role in Hmong marriages is the wearing of traditional Hmong dress for the betrothed couple and several individuals of the official marriage parties, including the bride's maid and the grooms' men. A significant artifact component that continues to be practiced is having the relatives and official marriage parties as witnesses to the union of the couple. Therefore, if a marriage should be in question as to the legalities according to the Hmong traditional practices, then these artifacts would be attested as evidence. Analyzing this perspective from a different angle unfolds a deeper level that the Hmong subcultures continue to uphold, perhaps to varying degrees, the norms, values, and assumptions of the culture regardless of personal preferences and choice.

Lawrence and Lorsch (1969) indicated that "It is no mystery that organizations must carry on transactions with their environment simply to survive, and, even more importantly, to grow" (p. 23), noting that, "As the relevant environment changes, however, organizations not only need suitable matched units, but on occasion also need to establish new units to address newly emerging environmental facts and to regroup old units" (p. 28). Furthermore, they stated that:

> An organization in which each of its boundary-spanning units is well matched with its corresponding environmental sector is in a desirable position to detect opportunities for new kinds of favorable transactions with the environment and to anticipate newly developing hazards in the environment. (p. 28)

The Hmong are a group of people who have been searching for and seeking an environment that promotes growth, development, and advancement while also tolerating cultural and traditional resiliency. The researcher's mother often said, "Coming to America is like a seed that has been planted in a well-fertilized soil. With the right amount of water and minimal care, the seed is bound to sprout and be fruitful" (Ka Mouavangsou, personal communication, June 24, 2008). The Hmong have what is known as an *open system*, which allows for both oscillation of their cultural organization and their new environment, which has definitely promoted growth and advancement.

Looking at the Hmong traditional marriage ceremony as a subculture, the Hmong are currently transitioning through Kurt Lewin's change model (Lewin, 1951) where there are three distinct stages of change: freeze, unfreeze, and refreeze. The unfreeze stage is where the organization has been comfortable in its current stage and now is beginning to have discomfort, which may lead to unfreezing and movement into the unfreezing stage. The traditional Hmong marriage ceremony ritual had been at a frozen stage while the Hmong lived in Laos and the refugee camps of Thailand. Since their migration to the United States, they were beginning to experience some discomfort in their new U.S. environment and culture. They were beginning to feel a "push" for change (Cummings & Worley, 2005, p. 22). Transitioning in and out of this stage depends largely on the number of years and acculturation and assimilation of the Hmong individuals who came to this country. The number of Hmong individuals transitioning out of this stage is perhaps those individuals who may be newcomer Hmong who have recently resettled in the United States, because the majority of the Hmong are probably in the movement stage where they are actively involved in making changes and modifications to the traditional marriage ceremonies (Cummings & Worley, 2005). In this stage, creativity for change is heightened. To illustrate the activities in this stage, a standard of practice for the bride price was preliminarily established through some brief discussions in the early 2000s about streamlining the bride price to $5,000.00. Although the bride price had preliminarily been established, many Hmong were still asking the groom for whatever amount of money that both sides of the families could agree upon during the marriage negotiation process. Until agreements on streamlining the traditional marriage ceremony are accepted and being practiced, the Hmong will most likely continue to operate in this stage for many more years before feeling the need of being pushed into the refreeze stage. Eventually, the Hmong will slowly enter into the refreeze stage if they have an agreed-upon standardized regulation involving marriage ceremony rituals with Hmong individuals who are consistently following the guidelines that have been set forth.

History and Culture of the Hmong

There are an estimated 4 to 5 million Hmong living in the world today, with a majority of them living in the southern provinces of China (Lemoine, 2005). There are about 3 million Hmong in China; approximately 450,000 in Laos; 790,000 in Vietnam; and 150,000 in Thailand (Quang, 2004). There are more than 30,000 Lao Hmong living along the Thai and Lao border (Hockings, 1993). It is estimated that there are about 186,000 Hmong living in the United States, according to the 2000 U.S. Census; however, there are some estimates that the number of Hmong living in the U.S. should be about 283,000, since there may be some Hmong who were not accounted for during the 2000 Census (Pfeifer & Lee, 2000; U.S. Census Bureau, 2000). The Hmong who are living in other countries are as follows: 15,000 in France; 1,800 in French Guiana; 640 in Canada; 1,860 in Australia; and 250 in Argentina (Lee & Tapp, 2007). According to Lemoine (2005), there are still about 320,000 Hmong who are in other resettlement countries throughout the world.

Ancient China

The Hmong are noted as one of the most ancient groups of people in the world (Dao, 1982). Despite recent studies being conducted to find the exact origin of the Hmong, the origin existence of the Hmong is still unknown. There are Hmong legends and folk tales that have highlighted the Hmong's historic journey from the dawn of time to the present. Some Hmong folk tales described a place where they once lived with 6 months of light and 6 months of darkness, where snow laid on mountains and lakes (Pfaff, 1995; Vang & Lewis, 1990). However, Dao (1982) stated that Hmong had cultivated the plains of the Blue River and the Yellow River in China. Chinese records mentioned the existence of the Hmong as *barbarians* between 1300 B.C. and 1200 A.D., while Pfaff (1995) related that the Hmong traveled eastward, descending through northeast Tibet into southern China. The Hmong are said to have lived in Szechwan, Yunnan, Hunan, and Kweichow Provinces in China since 2500 B.C. (Cerhan, 1990; Meyers, 1992; Pfaff, 1995).

Lemoine (2005) indicated that, according to more recent research, the Hmong predominantly live in Sichuan, Guizhou, Yunnan, and Guangxi, which extend from the northern region to the southern region of China bordering Vietnam (Lee & Tapp, 2007). Lemoine (2005) noted that the Hmong are an ethnic minority being grouped together under 1 of the 55 minority groups called "Miao" in China (p. 1). "The Chinese call us Miao; the groups in Indochina call us Meo; but we call ourselves Hmong" (Koumarn, 1978, p. 3). The Hmong are a highland tribal people who have enjoyed peace and harmony; they have chosen to live in remote villages, away from governmental rules. They are notable mountain-dwelling farmers, farming the highest ridges, upland valleys, and the steep mountain slopes of remote areas in Asia (Ng, 1995).

Since the Manchu Dynasty sought total control in the 17th century, they ordered the Han-Chinese settlers to scatter the

Hmong families by expanding slowly southward to the Hmong villages (Hockings, 1993; Pfaff, 1995). Suppressed further by the Chinese, the Hmong continued their journey southward until the 19th century (Cappelletty, 1986). Perhaps one of the most violent encounters that took place during the Chinese suppression was when the local troops called the Imperial Armies to quell a *Miao* uprising (Gonen, 1993). The Chinese tried to force the Hmong to give up their language, customs, dress, and way of life. Many of them refused, left China, and moved further south to seek peace and independence (Mickey, 1981; Vang & Lewis, 1990).

According to Cheon-Klessing, Camilleri, McElmurry, and Ohlson (1988), the Hmong migrated from China to other parts of Southeast Asia, including the northern region mountains of Myanmar (Burma), Laos, Thailand, Cambodia, and Vietnam (Meyers, 1992; Vang & Lewis, 1990). While the Hmong lived in their isolated villages at high-elevation in the mountains, they were temporarily free from colonial government interference (Koumarn, 1978). Regardless of their continual journey to seek peace in many lands, the Hmong have continually striven to preserve and defend their unique language, religion, and cultural heritage (Ng, 1995).

Journey to Laos

To further preserve their way of life, the Hmong took another journey to what the Hmong of China called *miv ntuj,* which means small world and what is now Southeast Asia (Xay Leng Mouavangsou, personal communication, August 1996). The group of Hmong in Southeast Asia is the one that the researcher focused on in this study and is from the Kingdom of Laos.

Laos is a landlocked, mountainous country with many isolated villages and few large cities. It is bordered by China, Vietnam, Cambodia, Thailand, and Myanmar (Burma). Because Laos is isolated from outside contacts and influences, it is thinly populated (Geography Department, 1996). The Hmong favored Laos because of its climate; Laos's cycle of rainy and dry seasons is similar to that in China (Vang & Lewis, 1990). With a population of 4.8 million in Laos, the Hmong are among 1 of the 68 minority groups that thrive on its tropical land (*Countries of the World: And Their Leaders Yearbook*, 1990).

When the Hmong first arrived in Laos, the vast majority of them settled in a plateau area called the Plain of Jars. To prevent confrontations with other people who had already inhabited the land, the Hmong scattered into small, multiple, and self-sufficient groups throughout the Xieng Khouang Province. There, they were able to cultivate the land and grow crops, raise livestock, and barter for goods that they could not obtain from the land (Pfaff, 1995). In their free society, the Hmong employed the slash-and-burn method for farming the lands (Cerhan, 1990; Dao, 1993). Fires were set to clear fields for planting, and the ash was used to fertilize the soil. As Steinbeck (cited in Schanche, 1970, p. vii) wrote:

> And where the hills are gentle enough so that a man does not fall off, the little fields of slash-and-burn agriculture can be seen from the air. The trees are cut and the brush slashed down and burned. Then the mountain farmer plants his rice. . . . The trees lying in careful patterns hold back eroding soil in the hard rainy season and draw and hold moisture in the dry. It is a haphazard wasteful way of staying alive, but is the only way the mountain people have.

This ancient method of cultivation was used to grow rice, corn, and opium fields. Rice was the main staple crop for the Hmong, while corn was mainly used as feed for domestic animals, such as chickens, pigs, and cattle. The opium poppies were used as a cash crop and for medicine (Cappelletty, 1986; Hockings, 1993). The Hmong also thrived on a good diet of vegetables and fruits from the countryside (Pfaff, 1995). They used horses both as a means of transportation and for transporting goods (Mouanoutoua, 1989). The Hmong had other common properties, such as musical instruments, cross-bows, Hmong-made flintlock guns, and tools for farming.

> Culas (2004) stated that
> The traditional agrarian economy of the Hmong is centered on the family rearing of pigs, poultry, buffalo, and goats; food crop cultivation (rice, corn, sweet potatoes, vegetables); . . . the Hmong cultivate poppies for opium, which is often their sole source of income. (p. 99)

They are a self-sufficient society resorting to interacting with outsiders for trading goods, such as fabrics, salt, sugar, and oil for cooking.

What Is Hmong?

Being Hmong means a host of descriptors, in particular having similarities in clothing, beliefs, community based with a collective consciousness, "living by certain commitment and social values," and "being in relationship with other people" (Lee, 1996, p. 6). In terms of being a Hmong at the individual level, certain characteristics, such as "one's birth and look, descent, given names, observance of particular religious beliefs, and one's identification or interactions with Hmong and other people" are similar (Lee, 1996, p. 6). Keown-Bomar (2004) indicated that being Hmong is having substance of Hmong such as "personal identity, codes of conduct, and relationships with others," and having terms of Hmong which include "dress, ritual, and language fluency" (p. 158).

According to Lee and Tapp (2007), both White Hmong and Green Hmong "belong to the same ethnic group by virtue of their common religious practices, history, cultural traditions and language [despite some dialect difference]" (p. 2). The most distinctive difference among Hmong groups is their dialects, which also correlate to the color of the women's skirts (Lee & Tapp, 2007).

Language

The Hmong language is a multitonal language of the Sino-Tibetan group (Conquergood, Thao, & Thao, 1989). There are two dialects in the Hmong language: White Hmong and Green Hmong. Although the dialects are slightly different, both groups can understand the other's dialect relatively well. Hmong has been an oral language for many centuries, and stories and folk tales have been passed on through word of mouth from one generation to the next. It was in the 1950s and 1960s that the Romanized alphabet was developed by French missionaries and thus the Hmong written language was born (Conquergood et al., 1989; Downing, 1986; Mouanoutoua, 1989).

Religion and Beliefs

The vast majority of the Hmong observe their traditional religious beliefs of Animism and Ancestral Worship. According to these traditional beliefs, spirits inhabit natural objects, animals, and some exist openly among humans. Other spirits include domestic ones that guard and protect the family welfare and well-being, such as the prosperity spirit (*xwm kaab*), doorway spirit, stove spirit, main house beam spirit, and fireplace spirit (Ka Xiong, personal communication, December 31, 2007). Some of the Hmong have converted to Christianity, especially since 1975 (Mua, 2002). The Hmong's beliefs have developed over the centuries (Ng, 1995), and they believe in the existence of good and bad spirits. "A third kind of spirit was called Neng, which was endowed with the power to fight evil spirits. The Neng spirit would choose people to be the host and taught them to diagnose and cure illness and ward off evil spirits" (Mouanoutoua,

1989, p. 15). Neng is called *neeb* in the Hmong native language. Neng is shamanism which is "not a religion but a way of healing" (Lemoine, 1986, p. 339).

According to shaman Ka Xiong (personal communication, December 31, 2007), a shaman who is chosen by the *qhua neeb* or Neng spirits had to undergo and endure long and sometimes deathly illnesses for an extended amount of time before a master shaman was able to ordain that person to be a shaman. The lengthy illness for the chosen individual could occur for months or even years until a healer could diagnose the cause of the illness. A shaman is a healer who travels between the human world and the spirit realm while in trance. Upon traveling to the spiritual world, the shaman is guarded and guided by her or his Neng spirits. The Neng spirits are similar to soldiers in the military, and the shaman is considered to be that of a general. In traveling to the spiritual world, the shaman makes contact with the spirit that caused illness and pain to the human individual. The shaman acts as an intermediator and pleads with the spirit to restore health and vitality to the human individual in return for offerings of spiritual money paper and animal sacrifice. Although shamans may have the gift of healing the sick through *ua neeb* or heal through Neng, some shamans also know how to cure illnesses with herbal remedies.

An herbal spirit healer or *dlaab tshuaj* may choose a person who is an herbalist. By having a *dlaab tshuaj*, the medicines given to the sick by the herbalist are believed to be potent and powerful enough to cure the illnesses. An herbal spirit chooses one person within a clan from one generation to the next to be a gifted herbalist. These herbalists remember remedies; they are often right about diagnosing the illness and giving the proper remedy for most of the diagnosed illnesses (Ka Xiong, personal communication, December 31, 2007).

Furthermore, Ka Xiong (personal communication, December 31, 2007) indicated that each person has three souls. These souls remain with the body while the person is still alive.

When a person dies, one of the souls goes to heaven or *sau ntuj* to be reborn, one stays with the body at the gravesite, and the third one stays with the children. The soul that remains at the graveside resides there until the body has completely decayed and then it rejoins the soul that has already been reborn into a new human form. The soul that remains with the children is called the *xyw*. This soul never leaves the family and remains with the children for all eternity.

The Hmong have a strong belief in the equilibrium between man and nature. Whenever an illness occurs, they believe it may be due to an unbalance of the human world and the spirit realm. They view illnesses as the result of natural, non-spiritual, or spiritual causes. The Hmong have several forms of remedies for different types of illnesses (Barney, 1981; Cheon-Klessing et al., 1988; Meyers, 1992; Thao, 1986). In their community, if a person is ill due to organic causes, Thao (1986) reported that herbal medicine will most likely be used to cure illnesses. If there is a magical and spiritual cause for the illness, the use of traditional rituals would be performed. There are people with special abilities to perform healings, depending on the cause of the illness (Bliatout, 1986).

In traditional medical practice, there are diagnosticians and healers. Not all healers are diagnosticians so referrals to healers would be made once a cause of the illness has been determined. Such diagnosticians are fortunetellers, egg readers, bean and rice readers, ear readers, basket talkers, and spoon talkers (Bliatout, 1986). There are multiple ways to cure illnesses. For example, an herbalist would use a variety of fresh and dried herbs to cure the illness. Massage is a technique that is being used to cure head, muscle, or stomach pains. Needle users are healers who use needles for acupuncture to release illnesses. Soul callers or *hu plig* are asked to call a person who may have lost his or her soul. The soul caller performs a ceremony or chants to call the soul to return to his or her body. Finally, a shaman or *txiv neeb* is called to go into the spirit world to find the cause of the illness.

The Hmong often call a shaman to help them maintain balance by performing ceremonies and sacrifices to the spirits that are causing the illnesses. They believe that the shaman can appease angry spirits or lead lost souls back to their bodies (McInnis, 1991). The shaman determines the cause of the illness then makes an offering to the spirit there. The illness may occur because the person has offended a spirit and it is demanding a payment in return. Sometimes it may be due to a relative who may be suffering from the spiritual world and that spirit is causing the person to be sick. In this case, the sick individual would ask the shaman to travel to the spiritual world to find the cause so that the sick individual could be healed. Oftentimes, the root of the illness may be because the person's soul is lost or is depressed or sad for some reason or another and the family may need to repent to the ill person so that the ill person's soul would return to the body (Ka Xiong, personal communication, December 31, 2007).

Social Organization and Relationships

The Hmong have maintained a high degree of social and political solidarity with cultural customs for centuries (Barney, 1981). They follow a patrilineal clan system (Meredith & Rowe, 1986a, 1986b).

> The clan system is based on the surname used by one's paternal kin group. A lineage is based on membership in descent line which can be traced to a known ancestor and a common set of ancestral rituals, while with a clan this is not possible beyond the sharing of a surname. (Lee & Tapp, 2007, p. 6)

The clan system in the Hmong social organization serves as a primary integrating factor in the Hmong culture as a whole (Barney, 1981). Mouanoutoua (1989) indicated that the clan system serves two purposes in the Hmong culture. First, it allows marriages to occur between two clans. And second, it acts as a collective mutual support system. A person becomes a member of a clan by being born into the clan. A child automatically becomes a member of his father's clan. When a young woman marries a man, she becomes a member of his clan and her identity is that of his family's (Cerhan, 1990; Meredith & Rowe, 1986a, 1986b). Keown-Bomar (2004) stated, "If a woman marries into another social group [clan] she is expected to adopt the dialect and the domestic and ceremonial patterns of her husband's family" (p. 46). The Hmong observed a brother-sister relationship among individuals with the same clan name; therefore, marriage among same clan name is strictly prohibited. Even if the two individuals have never met or have been separated by thousands of miles, they still adhere to this rule and can never marry one another (Cerhan, 1990; Cheon-Klessing et al., 1988; Keown-Bomar, 2004; Meredith & Rowe, 1986a, 1986b).

The patrilineal clan system of the Hmong ties social interactions, political affiliations, economic status, and religious practices that serve as the primary focus in the daily activities of the Hmong's life (Lewis & Lewis, 1984). Within the clan, there are skilled individuals who are healers, marriage brokers, teachers, and disciplinarians. "Clans offer security" (Fink, 1981, p. 24). "Clan identification serves as both a psychological and sociological indicator of belonging" (McInnis, 1991, p. 573). A person will seek a clan leader or family for supporting network or advice (Lin, Inui, Kleinman, & Womack, 1982; Nishio & Bilmes, 1987; Uba, 1992). The clan leader serves as the head of all families who belong to that clan. Members of the clan are often extremely loyal to each other (Cerhan, 1990).

Within the clan there is a kinship system. According to Keown-Bomar (2004), the kinship system is the heart of Hmong social organization and family life because they are from the same bloodline or ancestor and are extended members of the nucleus family. The Hmong observed an exogamous patri-clan (*xeem*) and lineage (*caaj ceg*) system as there are 18 patri-clans currently being recognized. The 18 recognizable clan names are the following: Chang (*Tsaab*), Cheng (*Tsheej*), Chue (*Tswb*), Fang (*Faaj*), Hang (*Haam*), Her (*Hawj*), Khang (Khaab), Kong (*Koo*), Kue (Kwm), Lee (*Lis*), Lor (*Lauj*), Moua (*Muas*), Pha (*Phaab*), Thao *(Thoj)*, Vang (*Vaaj*), Vue (*Vwj*), Xiong (*Xyooj*), and Yang (*Yaaj*).

The Village

The Hmong live in remote villages on top of misty mountains in Laos. The village is often sheltered by a belt of trees in a forest and has plenty of water sources (Hockings, 1993). The village location is often nearby the streams, which are flowing from the top of the mountains, so that water can easily be carried to the village with buckets or with aqueduct systems made from large bamboo stalks that are split lengthways (Cooper, 1998). There are anywhere from 20 to 40 families in a village, which is often comprised of the same clan and sometimes of a specific lineage. Because of this type of clan concentration, men often have to travel to other nearby villages to court women of different clans. A Hmong village is not fenced, nor does it have a main entrance gate to the village.

The House

Hmong houses were built with wood, bamboo, and other natural resources found in the area surrounding the villages. The Hmong used bamboo, grass, palm leaves, and wood shingles for roofing, while wooden pegs were used for the construction (Bonner & Chang, 1995). Mouanoutoua (1989) mentioned that Hmong houses were usually divided into two large rooms, with one being the family bedroom and the other the guest bedroom, an altar, and a dining area. Wealth and the composition of the household members may call for a larger house with multiple sleeping quarters (Cooper, 1998). Attics were made for storage of dry goods (The Hmong Youth Cultural Awareness Project, 1994). Due to their remoteness, homes did not contain running water or sewage systems (Bliatout, 1982). Hmong houses are often faced downward in one direction, forming a horseshoe-like pattern (Lewis & Lewis, 1984). The Hmong believed that the front door facing east or west is auspicious, as the sun will help awaken the family members in the early hours of the morning and bring good luck to the family (Ka Xiong, personal communication, December 17, 2007).

Family Structure

The family is considered the basic structure of the Hmong life (Manio & Hall, 1987). Patriarchy is practiced and an extended family is common. There is a strong sense of familial self, so the family takes precedence over the self. Children are taught to work together and be interdependent as opposed to independent (Meyers, 1992). Therefore, most decisions are made by the family as a group or clan. Within the immediate family, the eldest member of the family usually makes the final decisions for the family (Community Planning Organization, Inc., 1980; Hoang & Erickson, 1982). Respect for one another according to age is most important; the young must respect the old, and the old must have the utmost respect for the eldest of the family. Lewis and Lewis (1984) indicated that:

> Children respect their parents; younger siblings respect older siblings; nieces and nephews respect aunts and uncles, varying in degree according to their relative age. The father-son link is especially important. The father's welfare in the afterworld depends largely on the sumptuousness of the funeral ceremony given for him by his sons, and a son's welfare in turn is thought to depend on the respect he bestows on his parents while they are alive and on the treatment he receives from his deceased ancestors. (p. 124)

Oftentimes, the members of the household could be from 10 to 20 people as the sons marry and have children of their own (Lewis & Lewis, 1984). Cooper (1998) stated:

> There is no formal point at which a man leaves the parent household. When he does so, he will certainly be married and is most likely to have one or two children. If economic conditions permit, it is usual for a man to spend several years after marriage in his father's house before moving into a situation of independence. (p. 25)

Sometimes, the sons of a household would choose to remain in their parents house until the head of the household dies before they move out and live on their own; however, the mother continues to live with the youngest son. It is often the responsibility of the youngest son to take care of the mother after the father has died (Lewis & Lewis, 1984). It is not customary for an unmarried child to live alone regardless of age and gender (Ka Xiong, personal communication, December 31, 2007).

Traditional Gender Roles

In the Hmong society, the males often have more power in their roles than do the females. While the women can make suggestions on some decisions, most of the actual decisions are made by the men. The main role of the woman is to be responsible for household chores, child rearing, and agricultural activities. Men primarily have cared for the livestock, cleared fields, conducted trade, built and repaired houses, and held some specialized positions within the villages (Mouanoutoua, 1989). Traditional rituals and customs ceremonies are reserved for the men. Although there are some rituals that can be performed by either gender, most ancestral type rituals and ceremonies must only be performed by a male member of the household. For instance, the head of the household or the oldest son of the household must make offerings to the house spirits and ancestors when there is a feast in the home.

Mouanoutoua (1989) indicated that the Hmong were a preliterate society until the late 1930s. Only a limited number of young Hmong men were introduced to the Lao written language. In those times, only the wealthier families could afford to send a family member or two to schools in the city. Even in the 1960s and early 1970s, only a handful of women went to school and achieved graduation (Vang, 2008).

Hmong New Year

The Hmong followed the lunar calendar; however, they had no corresponding words for the English days of the week or months of the year. The Hmong indicated days of the week as Day One, Day Two, and so on. Similarly, they also referred to the months of the year as Month 1, Month 2, and so on. Mouanoutoua (1989) mentioned that the Hmong measured the time of the day by the inclining of the sun or the daily activities they would normally perform, such as "pig feeding time" or "the first crow of the rooster." They also measured distance by indicating that a certain place would take about half a day's walk. Similarly, seasons of the year were measured by the time of the year a certain crop was being planted or harvested.

The Hmong New Year marks the completion of harvest and a time to celebrate, to rest, and enjoy the company of families, relatives, and friends. Normally, the Hmong New Year is toward the end of the month in November. The Hmong called the New Year celebration *Noj Peb Caug*, which literally means Eat Thirty. It is a significant time to let go of the past year and welcome the New Year. There are specific rituals that are performed to begin a new year in every home. Every family in the village used a pair of chickens to *hu plig* or call the members of the family's souls back home. They believe that perhaps throughout the year, souls of family members may have wandered off and may not remember the way back to their human bodies. In addition, new special *ntawv nyaj* or special rice money papers are placed at doors, and *xwm kaab los yej* or the prosperity spirit located on a rice money paper altar is asked to take its place on the wall directly from the front door. Additionally, members of the *Dlaab Qhuas* or the house spirits are asked to bless, guard, and watch over the welfare and well-being of the household members for the coming year. When these rituals are completed, a (feast) special meal is cooked, and members of the village are asked to go from one house to another throughout the village to *noj peb caug* or feast in a New Year meal. Upon the completion of the *noj peb caug*, the villagers can begin the festive New Year celebration where young and old alike dress in their finest clothes and go to an open field in the village to play a game called *pov pob* or ball tossing.

The New Year celebration is a time for young men and women to *pov pob* and *has lug txaj* or toss ball with each other and sing traditional Hmong songs. This is the prime opportunity for young men and women to court openly and to find suitable husbands and wives. Through the game of *pov pob* and *has lug txaj*, young men and women would use eloquent and flowery words in their songs to express their feelings for one another (Symonds, 2004). It is often after the New Year that marriages occurred among the Hmong. Oftentimes, even the old are out in the *tshaav pov pob* or tossing ball field selecting suitable wives for their sons.

Courtship

Courtship among the young men and women was done during the night because affection for each other was to remain a secret between the two people (Mouanoutoua, 1989). Furthermore, Mouanoutoua stated that it was considered shameful for the woman's family if their relationship was known in public. Oftentimes, the man would have to find excuses to visit the woman. In addition, premarital sex was strongly controlled and pregnancy before marriage was a disgrace for the family (Faller, 1985; Meredith & Rowe, 1986a, 1986b).

The following passage, which described the courtship, was based on a personal communication with Xay Leng Mouavangsou in 1996:

The Hmong is modest by nature. Young men and women are instructed to be modest and quiet. The relationship between a man and a woman is kept as a secret. Interactions and intermingling of young men and women often occurred during the celebration of the New Year. If a young man is interested in courting a young woman, he would go to the young woman's home in the late evening when she was finished with her chores and all of the other members of the household would be fast asleep. The young man would go to the outside of the young woman's sleeping quarters and tap on the outside wall to awaken her to converse with him. Because Hmong houses are made with thin bamboo planks, it is easy to communicate quietly without being heard by the young woman's family members. Oftentimes, the young man would stay until the early hours of the next morning where the dew had already collected on the young man's jacket. Since members of the same clan tend to live in one village, young men would have to walk long distances to different villages to court young women. A young man would carry a flash light or sometimes a burning torch to help him see along the way. He sometimes needed to walk many miles at night to reach the young woman's village.

Sometimes, the young woman and man would use a Jew's harp called *ncaas* to communicate their love for each other (Symonds, 2004). Because the young individuals are usually shy and modest, it would be less embarrassing to express love for one another with the *ncaas* than to actually openly express their feelings for one another.

It is considered inappropriate for the young man to go inside the young woman's home for courtship. According to

Cooper (1998), it would anger the house spirits if sex occurred between any unmarried couple inside of any house.

Marriage

The Hmong's traditional marriage ceremony is an institution that provides a venue for interactions between two individuals' families and clans. Marriage between two people is more than just a bond between two people and their immediate families; it is considered to be a bridge between two clans that connects and ties kinships.

> A Hmong marriage is far more than a union between two people; it is one of a series of unions between clans and lineages. Marriage not only facilitates new alliances and family networks but repairs old alliances through the resolution of past disagreements. (Symonds, 2004, p. 40)

Marriage arrangements for the Hmong occur in several forms, such as mutual consent, elopement, kidnapping, or forced and arranged. According to Bertrais (1978), the following are four of the ways that the Hmong become married:

1. Mutual consent: The bride and the groom request their parents' permission to marry, and the negotiations are favorable for both, especially the bride.

2. Elopement: Both bride and groom happily want to marry each other and so the bride goes with the groom to his home, and a brief ritual to welcome her soul into the groom's family is performed.

3. Bride captured or kidnapped: The bride does not agree to marry the groom, but the groom kidnaps the bride against her will to marry him.

Another type of marriage arrangement is forced marriage. According to Bla Neng Vang (personal communication, March

20, 2007), the couple are forced to marry each other due to out-of-wedlock pregnancy or because they had offended or shamed the bride's family. Sometimes, they are forced to marry because they were caught courting out late in the night or sleeping together at the bride's home.

Even though there are several types of marriage arrangements, most of the rituals, songs, and ceremonies are the same. These forms of marriage arrangement practices have been used for thousands of years over the centuries, especially for arranged marriages. Because there are inequalities among gender and generations in the Hmong society, marriage could only be initiated by the man, and the woman has to submit to her husband and his parents after the marriage ceremony (Kunstadter, 2004).

Kunstadter (2004) stated, "Marriage in Hmong society joins the labor and reproductive capacity of the bride with the extended family household of the groom, and establishes or strengthens a union between extended families of the bride and groom" (p. 376). Additionally, Kunstadter stated that:

Two extended families are involved in any marriage, and actions of any member of the extended family affect the reputation of all other members. Marriage is seen as a time when any debts, arguments or offenses between the two families should be resolved. Because of the concern with reproduction, both families must be assured before the marriage that neither has a history of disease traditionally believed to be "inherited," especially Hansen's Disease (leprosy). (p. 376)

As discussed in the previous section, traditional Hmong marriage practices play a vital role in the Hmong's social relatedness through their lineage and kinship system. Keown-Bomar (2004) stated that, "Unlike other cultural understandings of kinship, the Hmong notion of being related is about socially established ties, not necessarily descent, genetic relatedness, or nurturance" (p. 14). The Hmong's social interaction is based on relatedness. When two people meet, they normally try to establish relatedness as a basis for addressing each other. Oftentimes, ulterior motives are behind the marriage rather than love between the two individuals. A marriage may occur for economic purposes, to strengthen the alliance between the clans, and sometimes for political reasons.

"The marriage ritual and the exchanges that accompany it assures participants that a couple's personal duty to continue the male matrilineal will be fulfilled" (Symonds, 2004, p. 71). Keown-Bomar (2004) stated that:

> Hmong men still assume these political and religious duties in the household. Because ancestral rites can only be performed by descending males, if there are no sons in the family, a lineage will be forgotten. As a result, many Hmong parents stress having one son or more to ensure the lineage and the physical and spiritual well being of the "tsev neeg" or family.
>
> (p. 51)

Polygamy has been a common practice among the Hmong and has been accepted as a form of marriage (Mouanoutoua, 1989). Part of the reason for acceptance of polygamy is due to the gender and generational inequalities in the Hmong society (Kunstadter, 2004). It is permissible for the man to continue to court other women even though he is married and may even take on additional wives if he chooses, but the wife has to remain monogamous (Kunstadter, 2004).

Traditionally, polygamy was viewed as a symbol of wealth since the man has to be wealthy to have multiple wives and provide for all their well-being. Several factors contributed to having several wives in Laos. One of the reasons for taking a second wife would be due to the death of an elder brother. When an older brother died, the younger brother would marry the older brother's widow. Sometimes, neither the younger brother nor the older brother's widow have any say in the marriage arrangement. There is no bride price for marrying the elder brother's widow since the bride price was already paid to the family when she married into the family (Lewis & Lewis, 1984). Another reason for marrying a second wife was the infertility of the first wife. A man wants to marry a second wife to produce children and heirs. In this case, the man's wife may play an active role in searching for a suitable second wife for her husband. When an agreement is reached between the wife and her husband regarding who he should marry, then an arrangement for the marriage is made. Another reason for marrying a second wife is that the man may want to establish ties with another clan for political reasons or to gain greater wealth or status in the village (Lewis & Lewis, 1984). Because marrying a wife is costly, not to mention the expense to ensure that all the wives live comfortably, most oftentimes only wealthy families could afford to have a son marry multiple wives.

Divorce was rarely practiced among the Hmong in Laos. It was looked upon as negative, and the community did not accept divorces easily. There were few divorces in the Hmong marriages because of a belief in the strong tie and unity of the two clans in a marriage. A divorce would mean problems for future marriages between the two clans. Their social system also provided for strong pressure for the couple to stay together regardless of conflicts and problems in the marriage (Mouanoutoua, 1989). Whenever a divorce occurred, most oftentimes it would be initiated by the man, and the children would stay with the husband's clan (Hockings, 1993; McInnis, 1991).

Any woman wanting to divorce her husband found that it was difficult. *"Yog has tas nqaj dluag ntshaav nrug ces peb maam nrug koj has."* This was a typical phrase made by the elders when a woman requested a divorce from her husband. Basically, the old saying stated that unless there is blood shed or a skin wound, there would be no discussion about a woman's request to divorce her husband. When a woman marries, her physical being and soul belong to her husband and are under the protection of her husband's ancestors. This is why there are so many Hmong taboos, especially those that apply for the Hmong women.

A man normally would not divorce his wife; he simply would have continual affairs or marry another wife. Keown-Bomar (2004) indicated that in Laos, a woman who has affairs would be divorced, scorned, and isolated, but a man who has extramarital affairs was not thought of as having affairs unless the affair was with a married woman. In this case, the man would have to involve his kinship to resolve the situation where a large amount of money would be at stake and perhaps losing face for the behavior. A husband having affairs does not justify a wife's wish to divorce him. A husband having an affair is considered irrelevant because it does not disrupt the stability of the family. A woman who has an affair jeopardizes the stability of the family, brings shame to the family name, is being disrespectful of her husband, and is viewed as a *bad wife* or *ib tug qos puj tsis zoo*. The husband in this case can divorce his wife based on infidelity.

Traditional Hmong Marriage Ceremony Rituals

To provide a better understanding of the institution of Hmong traditional marriage and the complexity of the Hmong marriage ceremony rituals in Laos, the researcher has provided a brief descriptive summary of each ceremony ritual to clarify and provide background information about the rituals and their significance in the marriage ceremony in Appendix A. The brief summaries will also help to better understand the findings that are presented in Chapter 4.

Much of the information provided throughout this study is based on personal communications with the researcher's father, Xay Leng Mouavangsou (August 1996), Bla Neng Vang (March 20, 2008), and Ka Xiong (December 31, 2007). Xay Leng Mouavangsou and Bla Neng Vang have also been prominent *mejkoob* or marriage go-betweens in Laos, Thailand, and in the USA.

There are some variations on the traditional marriage ceremony rituals and individuals involved throughout the marriage ceremony, depending on whether the bride is a White Hmong, *Moob Dlawb*, or Green Hmong, *Moob Ntsuab* or *Moob Leeg*. A superstitious and auspicious factor in the Hmong marriage ceremonies is related to even numbers and having pairs throughout the marriage ceremony from individuals in the marriage ceremony to ritual cups of drinks. The Hmong believe that having an even number in a marriage ceremony is important since the bride and the groom make a pair or the number 2. Because of this belief, White Hmong have two *mejkoob* because they do not have the *aub nraa* or the Marriage Lunch Basket carrier in the groom's official marriage party to even out the individuals to a total of six persons. In the Green Hmong's official marriage party from the groom's side, they only have one *mejkoob* because they include the *aub nraa* to make an even number of six individuals in the party.

An additional difference for the two types of Hmong is based on dialect and the contents found in the Marriage Lunch Basket. White Hmong have oils, salt, knife, two pairs of chicken feet, raw and cooked rice, and spoons in their baskets, while Green Hmong only require two pairs of chicken feet and occasionally some salt. Because the two groups marry each other interchangeably over the years, some of the Green Hmong are beginning to adopt some of the contents of the White Hmong's Marriage Lunch Basket.

Another difference between the two groups is the placement of the Marriage Umbrella at the bride's home. The Green Hmong require that the Marriage Umbrella be placed on the ground with the top pointing up to the prosperity spirit paper wall, while the White Hmong require that the Marriage Umbrella be hung on a beam in the *hauv taag* or on the north wall in the living room.

The *hu plig* or soul calling of the bride to the groom's home is also different between the two groups. While the White Hmong perform both the *hu plig* and *nqee plig* for the bride at the groom's home, the Green Hmong only do the *nqee plig* or the use of a chicken to welcome the bride's soul into the groom's family at the door and not the *hu plig* at all.

Another contingency that can slightly vary the marriage ceremony ritual is the actual type of marriage arrangement. Arranged marriage and mutual consent marriage types of arrangements tend to be lengthy due to the number of rituals involved in the marriage ceremony. Elopement and kidnaped or forced marriage arrangements have shorter ceremonies because there are less rituals involved.

To illustrate the complexities of traditional Hmong marriage ceremonies and an understanding of the marriage ceremony process, a story is presented. Larry B. Anders (1999) stated:

> To be a member of an organization is to have a story to tell. Stories can be stimulating and fun and reflect the spirit of the organization. They can offer memories of the past and serve as preparation for the future. There are no good or bad stories. And no right or wrong way to tell them. (p. 4)

The purpose of the story is to provide a basic foundation of the Hmong traditional marriage ceremony rituals in Laos and in some cases in the U.S. as a way to highlight the factors that result in changes to the traditional marriage ceremony rituals.

The following story was told to the researcher by one of her aunts based on the Green Hmong's way of marriage through elopement. This story took place in the mystical mountains of Laos many years ago during the aunt's youthful years.

It was after the Hmong New Year at the village of Na Fen, Laos, that Shoua Thao decided that he wanted to settle down and start a family with a girl he recently met. Although he had just met May Xiong, he already knew that he had met the girl who would be his wife. Since Shoua lived in a far away village, he had to walk many miles after working in the field to court May at her village. It was during the spring season when all plant life has begun to bud and bloom that Shoua decided he would ask May to marry him.

Since both Shoua and May had already agreed to marry each other, they decided that May would go with Shoua to his home. May noticed that Shoua brought along two relatives when he came over to her house that night. May knew that these two elders were going to inform her parents about their elopement. As soon as Shoua and May left for his home, Shoua's two relatives knocked on May's parents' front door to *thoob xu* or inform them of the marriage.

When May and Shoua got back to Shoua's home, his parents were ready with a live chicken in hand to greet them. Upon May entering Shoua's front door, Shoua's aunt used the chicken to circle over May's head three times to welcome her soul to Shoua's family. May was told by Shoua's aunt to not walk into anyone else's home for the next 3 days since it was one of the ways of the Hmong to restrict oneself to only the groom's home within that time frame. May recalled being the age of 16 and Shoua was 20 years old.

May said that her parents told her that they were surprised when a couple of the men came to their home to *thoob xu* or inform them about Shoua and May's elopement. May's parents asked one of their elder cousins, Tong Kua, to be the *Txiv Tsawb Tshoob* for the *thoob xu* process. At the *thoob xu*, Shoua's two elders presented two pinches of chopped cigarette leaves to May's mother and father, and the elders who came to the *thoob xu* along with *ob npib*, which is equivalent to about $1.00 in U.S. dollars. Shoua's elders told the *Txiv Tsawb Tshoob* that the young couple had decided to marry and that May's parents should not worry about May's whereabouts. Although sad, May's parents accepted the elopement of their daughter by taking the money and the cigarette leaves. After the *thoob xu*, Shoua's elders sat with the *Txiv Tsawb Tshoob* to discuss the marriage ceremony day. Everyone agreed that it would be the *lub 4 hlis ntuj nu*b tim 8 or April 8th. After the agreement, the two elders left the home. May's parents continued to have discussions with the *Txiv Tsawb Tshoob* around the *qhov cub* or main hearth to share stories and past experiences of marriages. They knew that there would be a great deal of preparation ahead for the marriage ceremony of their daughter May to Shoua.

As the day for May to visit her parents grew near, May got excited. This was the first time that May had been away from her parents, and she missed her parents very much. On the other hand, Shoua was nervous since he knew that upon visiting May's parents, Shoua would have to play the role of know-it-all son-in-law when asked to perform chores and tasks.

Although May was finally allowed to visit her family, this was no ordinary visit since May was now considered a guest of her own home. May's family was busy preparing for Shoua's and May's visit days prior to their visitation by slaughtering some chickens and harvesting some fresh vegetables from their corn field. A new bed made of bamboo planks was also placed near the living room of their home for May and Shoua.

After 3 days, Shoua's parents told Shoua to take May to visit her parents and to spend the night at May's home. Upon arriving at May's home, her parents were happy to see May, especially May's mother. She embraced May and told May that she had missed her very much in the last 3 days. The next morning, May's parents slaughtered a chicken and boiled it to pack for Shoua's and May's lunch as they headed back home.

Both Shoua's and May's families were quite busy for the next month and a half thatchering and winding enough rice for the marriage ceremony. At time, they even had the neighbors help pound rice grains so that there would be plenty of rice for the feasts. Also, because the marriage ceremony would call for alcohol, both families made multiple barrels and jars of rice wine for the celebration. Similarly, both families were busy every evening making wood spoons. Shoua's parents had to round up some of their best chickens and pigs as there would be multiple meals that needed to be prepared throughout their children's marriage ceremony celebration.

A couple of days prior to the day of the marriage ceremony, Shoua's parents had to ask relatives in their village to assume the roles of the official marriage ceremony party. Shoua and his father went to one of the prominent elders in the village who had been a *mejkoob* or marriage go-between for Shoua's Uncle Cheng's marriage ceremony 5 years ago. Fortunately, Chang Fue was home that evening, relaxing and smoking his pipe outside of his home. Upon Shoua's and his father's visit, Chang Fue invited them into his home. They sat around the main hearth and discussed Shoua's upcoming marriage ceremony. When Shoua's father asked Chang Fue to be the *mejkoob* for Shoua's marriage ceremony, Chang Fue humbly accepted the role. Shoua and his father got up and kneeled twice to thank Chang Fue for accepting the role of *mejkoob* for Shoua's marriage ceremony. After this, they continued to talk about May's relatives and their relationship to Shoua's relatives. Some discussions also revolved around earlier marriage ceremony experiences, wrong-doings between their relatives and other clans.

At last, the day came for Shoua and May to go to May's home for the marriage ceremony. That morning, May had to get up early to help prepare a feast for Shoua's relatives before they left for May's parents' home. The relatives also blessed the official marriage ceremony party for a safe journey to and from May's home and wished the marriage ceremony to be pleasant, harmonious, and smoothly celebrated.

It was customary for the mother-in-law and father-in-law to dress the bride in their finest clothes, as she returns home to celebrate the marriage, so Shoua's mother dressed both May and May's bride's maid, Pa, in the two newly sewed outfits for the journey to May's home. After May and Pa got dressed, they joined the rest of the official marriage party in the living room. Shoua and his best man, Seng, stood with their backs to the main front door, which was opened and *pe* or kneeled twice to all the house spirits, Shoua's ancestors, parents, uncles, elders of his kinship, and the rest of the individuals who had come to the feast that morning. Upon completing this ritual, the official marriage ceremony party started their walk to May's home. The distance to May's home was a half-day's walk. The official marriage party on Shoua's side included Shoua's younger sister, Pa, who was the *nam ua luag* or the bride's maid; Shoua's cousin, Seng, who was the *pij laaj* or best man; Shoua's other cousin, Tou, who was the *aub nraa* or the one who carries the Marriage Lunch Basket; and Chang Fue, who was the *mejkoob* or the marriage go-between person.

About half way to May's home, the groom's official marriage party stopped to have lunch. Before eating the lunch, Chang Fue had to take a little bit of cooked rice and boiled chicken away from the party to offer it to the spirit who guards the area for protection and safe passage. They could eat all parts of the boiled chickens except for the feet. These chicken feet are the vital items, since they will be checked by May's official marriage party at May's home when they arrive.

When Shoua's official marriage party arrived at May's home, May's parents had already had a huge feast with her relatives prior to their coming. Upon their arrival, Chang Fue asked May's parents for the main door of May's home. Then, Chang Fue had Shoua and Seng *pe* twice to each person when Chang Fue called out their formal names, beginning with May's grandparents, mother and father, father's older and younger brothers and their wives, older and younger brothers, male first cousins, father's sisters and their husbands, and finally the house spirits of May's home. From there, Chang Fue walked over to the *xwm kaab* or prosperity spirit, which is a plain rice money paper on a wall directly across from the front door, and placed the Marriage Umbrella leaning against the wall with the tip pointing up.

After that, May's parents reset the feast table and invited Shoua's official marriage party to dine prior to conducting the marriage negotiations. While they were eating, the *kaav xwm* or master of ceremony had taken the lunch basket from Seng and put it down next to the main hearth of the house. The Marriage Lunch Basket indeed had all the necessary items, including two pairs of chicken feet and some salt, when May's family and the *kaav xwm* checked it. Later that evening, the table for the marriage negotiation was set in the middle of the living room for the two *mejkoob* to negotiate the bride price along with any other items of discussion between the two clans. Shoua's official marriage party sat around in the living quarters while May's family and relatives were in the bedroom along with May and Pa. Pa understood that her primary role was to guard May against any negative influence from her relatives and especially her mother or old boyfriends. Pa essentially was May's bride's maid in name, but a shadow in truth.

Meanwhile Shoua's other relatives, including Shoua's Uncle Tong Pao, who was Shoua's father's older brother, representing Shoua's father had also traveled to May's village. Since Shoua's official party's only privacy was outside of May's home, the front porch became the meeting quarters for Shoua's official marriage party, including Shoua's relatives and uncle.

During the negotiation process, it turned out that there had not been any marriage between the Thao clan and the Xiong clan within these two kinships. Because of this, it was deemed that a *choj tshoob* or a marriage bridge between the two clans needed to be established prior to further discussion of the marriage negotiations. The marriage bridge was negotiated for *10 npib* or about $5.00 U.S. dollars. After 2 hours of negotiations about the *nqe taubhau* or bride price, a consensus was reached that May's bride price would be *10 choj* or 10 silver bars, which was equivalent to about $1,000 U.S. dollars. Additionally, since May's older sister had not been married yet, another negotiated price of *20 npib* or $10 U.S. dollars was given to May's older sister, Youa. The money was given to Youa to *qhwv hauv caug* or cover her knee literally. In actuality, the money was exchanged to ask permission from Youa to allow May to marry first. Although difficult for Youa to accept the money from May's husband since the more money Shoua spent on the marriage ceremony, the less May and Shoua would have to start their life together without, she accepted it anyway. She knew that she could not refuse because this was the rule of the Hmong marriage tradition.

After this, long discussions continued about the marriage celebration ceremony for the next couple of days. It was agreed that Shoua's family would slaughter a pig the size of six fists around the roundest part of the pig, no more and no less, to host the marriage ceremony feast the next day. Early the next morning, Shoua's relatives had already brought the *npuas luam xwm*, which measured exactly six fists around the pig. This pig would be slaughtered for a feast to celebrate the marriage between May and Shoua. It took all morning to cook the many dishes from the pig and the chickens that May's parents helped provide for the feast. This meal is the biggest feast since all of May's relatives and members of May's village would attend and participate in the festivities and the celebration of the marriage.

After the main feast, the marriage ceremony rituals began. The official members of May's marriage party along with Shoua and his official marriage party were asked to sit around the marriage table. May's official marriage party included *yawm txoo* or May's father's older brother, *nam txiv dlaab* or May's mother's brother, *nam ntxawm txiv ntxawm or* May's father's younger brother, *nug tij* or May's older brother, and *tais laug txiv laug* or May's older sister and her husband. May's official marriage party were asked to take their place first. One by one, their formal names were called, and each person had to go down on his or her knees and drink the *cawv xwm* or the drink from a bowl along with a small cup of alcohol and another small cup with tea. When the person was finished with his or her drinks, he or she was permitted to take his or her chair at the marriage table. Shoua's party was on one side of the table, while May's official party was on the other side facing the door. Shoua noticed that Chang Fue was no longer sitting on his side of the table but rather on the other side with May's party. But then he remembered that it was customary for the *mejkoob* to switch sides to ensure the fairness of the rituals. When everyone was finished with their drinks and were seated in their rightful places, the official marriage rituals began.

Although Shoua had been tired from the earlier festivities, he knew that today would be the most important day. There would be many sequential rituals that involved drinking pairs of small alcohol cups until the end of the marriage ceremony rituals. Shoua had been preparing himself for today by having several plans in mind. Shoua, Seng, and Tou had worked out a plan to have Seng and Tou drink as much of the alcohol as possible so that Shoua would not be drunk at the end of the ceremony. Also, Shoua knew that if he should start to feel light headed or drunk, Tou would step in for Shoua as the groom, since it was permissible to replace the groom with another person if the groom was too drunk to continue.

As the first round of drinks began, Shoua realized that this round of drinks was to greet the guests or the *cawv txais qhuas*. In this case, Shoua and everyone at the table were considered guests. From this first round of drinks to the last, Shoua counted 15 rounds. He was thankful that Tou, Seng, and his relatives were there to help him with the drinks. Being a groom was no easy task since he was mandated to sit at the marriage table throughout the entire marriage ceremony with some relief from Tou every now and then. The *cawv theem tsum* or the postponed drink was the last round of drinks for that evening.

That night, most of the members of May's village came to May's home to celebrate. May's house was filled with eating competitions, such as *noj qaj npua rog* or eating cooked fat pork

and *noj mov txug* or rice eating contest. Young and old were
involved in singing competitive traditional songs or *lug txaj sib
lwv* except for May. As a bride, she was not allowed to take part
in this type of entertainment, although Shoua and Pa were
permitted to take part in the games. All the entertainment needed
to be joyful and jolly. Anyone who did not know how to sing
traditional songs or *has lug txaj* got a drink or did not want to eat
the fat pork or rice, they could sing a traditional song. That
evening was filled with many events and activities, which
followed into the early hours of the next day.

Early the next morning, the marriage rituals were nearly
done. After breakfast, the marriage table was set up with another
four rounds of drinks, which began with the *cawv tshais* or the
breakfast drink and ended with the *cawv fuam cum* or the
conclusion drink.

While the rituals at the marriage table resumed, May and
Pa were told to be dressed in the finest traditional Hmong outfits
given to them by May's mother and father. When they finished
dressing, May's mother, brothers, aunts, uncles, and cousins came
into the same bedroom to *qhuab nthuag* or talk to May about her
new responsibilities and duties as a daughter-in-law and wife.
As she listened to the wise words from her relatives, May realized
that this would be the last time that she would sit in her parents'
bedroom as their unwedded daughter. May knew that from this
day on, her physical being and spiritual soul would belong to
Shoua and his family. Her uncles and aunts shared their sadness
in losing her to another family and the emptiness that they would
feel by not having her present like she was before. They also
told her that this marriage was a one-way ticket into the life of a
married person and that there was no turning back. May and her
relatives all cried as they shared their innermost thoughts and
feelings with one another.

It was then that Shoua finally came into the bedroom
and told May and Pa to come into the living room. May was
asked to speak about whether she had any gifts from any old

boyfriends or not. Because May had never really courted anyone before Shoua, she did not have anything to report.

After that, Chang Fue stood by the door with May's *mejkoob* and sang a special song asking for the return of the Marriage Umbrella. When May's *mejkoob* gave Chang Fue the Marriage Umbrella, he thanked May's *mejkoob* for a smooth marriage ceremony celebration and the hospitable usage of May's home for the past couple of days. Chang Fue asked Shoua and Seng to kneel twice to May's parents, aunts and uncles, male relatives, grandparents, and the domestic house spirits to thank them for being hospitable and accommodating. Right before they left May's home, Shoua went up to May's mother and kneeled twice to her to pay his respects and thanked her for allowing him to marry May. Shoua also kneeled twice to May's father.

After that, Chang Fue walked out of May's home first and stood by the front door waiting for the rest of the groom's party to follow. While Shoua was leaving May's home, May's relatives were taking turns acquainting themselves with Shoua by giving him two small cups of alcohol each time they introduced themselves. Shoua barely made it out the door because May's relatives kept pouring him drinks. As soon as all the members of the party left May's house, Chang Fue took a preboiled chicken and tore it into two halves. He gave the half without the head to May's *mejkoob* for May's mother and took the one with the head for May. This was a symbolic ritual as it represents the separation of mother and daughter. From this moment forward, May and her mother would live separate lives with an equal amount of balance in life and spirit.

On their way back to Shoua's house, all the members of the marriage party were drunk, and Shoua's relatives had come to help the party home. May was the only one who was not drunk and though she was the only one with a clear mind, it was full of uncertainties. Starting a new life with a new family was going to be challenging, even though she had been trained well on the roles and duties of a dutiful daughter-in-law and wife at a young age.

Half way back home, the party had to stop for lunch. Sure enough, May's family had packed lunch for them, including all the necessary items in the Marriage Lunch Basket, along with doubling the spoons to four. Change Fue, again, took a small piece of chicken and rice to give offerings to the spirit of the area where they were having lunch.

For some reason, the journey back home was a lot quicker than when they walked to May's home. Perhaps it was because of all the activities that occurred at May's home and the words of her relatives that kept lingering on in her mind. As soon as they entered the outer boundaries of Shoua's village, it was evident that Shoua's parents and relatives had been anxiously awaiting their return.

A large group of relatives and members of Shoua's village were waiting outside of Shoua's home for them. As soon as Chang Fue knocked on the door, two elders inside of Shoua's home greeted them with eight small alcohol cups and asked them some questions regarding their whereabouts and who the master of the house was before they were allowed to enter the home. Upon entering the home, Chang Fue sang a special blessing marriage song to Shoua's family prior to drinking the four cups of alcohol. After Chang Fue drank the four cups, the other two elders drank the other four cups. A long table with food was ready for them when they walked inside. May and Pa walked directly to the bedroom while the rest of the members were asked to sit around the table.

It was during this time that Chang Fue recalled the details about the marriage ceremony celebration at May's home. He also shared information about the gifts and monies that were given to May and Shoua by May's parents and relatives. After that, one of Shoua's elders was asked to lead the *tam mejkoob* or thanking the go-between and the members of the marriage party for helping in the completion of the marriage ceremony for Shoua and May.

From there, Chang Fue asked May to join Shoua at the table for blessings by the elders around the table. Chang Fue was the first to bless May and Shou by wishing them a long life together filled with many children, good fortune, strong health, peace, and harmony. He then gave the Marriage Umbrella to Shoua's father and mother while blessing them as well. Chang Fue told Shoua's parents to keep the Marriage Umbrella in the bedroom for 3 days before opening it. After 3 days, Shoua's parents, along with May and Shoua, opened the Marriage Umbrella and unfolded all the blessings that were bestowed unto them as they began a fulfilled and prosperous life together.

The previous story was told as a sage way to better understand the traditional Hmong marriage ceremony ritual steps of a traditional Green Hmong marriage ceremony including both sides of the bride and the groom. As indicated earlier, Hmong marriage ceremonies are filled with complex proverbs, marriage songs, and rituals. Traditionally, there are anywhere from 4 to 22 or more marriage songs that may be sung throughout the marriage ceremony. However, only one of the marriage songs is provided as a sample. This marriage song is sung by the *mejkoob* on the groom's side when the bride's parents agree to give their daughter's hand in marriage to the groom. Additionally, since it takes a number of people to assist in the marriage negotiation process, the groom's *mejkoob* will sing a marriage song to accept the marriage and thank the bride's cousins for assisting in the marriage process and for being influential in persuading the bride's parents in approving the marriage. This song is significant as the groom's *mejkoob* acknowledges the bride's cousins for assisting and helping the negotiation processing and for sealing the marriage between the bride and the groom.

The following traditional Hmong marriage song to seal the approval of the couple's marriage was sung by the researcher's father, Xay Leng Mouavangsou, who was a prominent *mejkoob*.

Ib loj vis sawv ua tsaug
Peb ib txoom npoj kev txwj yuav tub tsheej vis npoj
kev yog
Nam nkaug los miv nkaug, nkaug lis nkuav tuaj qaab tsua
ntaab ca lawg kw
Phaaj nyaag lis tag lis suav tshoob, suav tshoob lis
tag qeg suav khwg es

Loj vis sawv ua tsaug nis txoog xeeb
Npoj kev txwj yuav txoog vis npoj kev laug
Mej tsua tuaj paab nyas laag yau ib luj ncej tshoob
nrooj khwg kos ca lawg kw
Nam nkaug ntos miv nkaug, nkaug lis nkuav tuaj qaab
roob ntoj vis ua tsaug
Mej ib tsoom npoj kev txij lis kev laug yuav tuaj lug
paab laag yog
Ib lub txheej lub paaj tshoob kuas ca lawm kws es

Muaj nub dlej laug dlwg tsi sis cuag, zoov laug hlaav
tuaj tsi sis ib los tseg
Dlwg lis ndlo ib kuab dlej ces ca lawg kw es
Muaj nub mej paaj tshoob kev khwg cig li yeev tuaj txug
laag yog ib tej ntug zog
Ib yuav ncu quas ntsoov mej kaum ob lub moog yeeb kooj
es tsi pub kuam tu os

Muaj nub dlej laug dlwg tsi sis cuag los tseg, zoov
laug txaav tsi sis ib los tseg
Dlej laug dlwg sis cuag zoov lawg hlaav sis ib ces
Dlwg lis dlos ua ib puab feej ces, laag yau ib yuav
ncu lis ntsoov mej ib tsoom npoj
Kev txwj yuav tsoom npoj kev laug kau
Ob lub moog yeeb txheej yuav tsi kuam txeej les ca
lawg kw ca lawg kw

*Muaj nub mej lis txoog xeeb npoj kev txwj yuav txoog
    lis npoj kev laug les*
*Mej tsua paaj tshoob kev khwg, nrov nreeg laag yau ib
    tej qaw zej ni*
Ib tsua ua nyog mej tub rov tos ntsej yuav ca lawg kws
*Muaj nub mej le paaj tshoob kev khwg tsua nrov nreeg
    tsis txug los yog*
*Ib tej qaws tug zog los tseg, paaj tshoob kev khwg nrov
    nreeg los yog ib tej tug zog,*
Ib yuav ca nyog mej tub rov to nrog ni

*Ntsai mej yeej cuam tsi txug los, yog ib los tseg yeej
    cuam txug los yog ib yuav tuaj paab*
*Ib yuav tuaj nrug mej cheem tshoob li paaj tshoob kev
    khwg rov nreeg los*
Yog ib tej qaws ntug zog ni
*Mej yeej cuam tsi txug laag yog ib los tseg yeej cuam
    laag yog*
*Ib ces qeg tuaj txug ib yuav tuaj cheem tshoob coj
    cheem khwg.*
(Xay Leng Mouavangsou, personal communication,
August 1996)

The following is a brief, translated summary of the traditional Hmong marriage song. The groom's marriage go-between indicated that they thank the bride's relatives for coming to the marriage negotiation ceremony to obtain the bride's parents' approval for the marriage. If someday, the bride's relatives should marry someone from the groom's village, the groom's marriage go-between would be willing to take part in the negotiation process of the marriage arrangement from beginning to completion if they should be called upon to help.

Essential artifacts are needed in order for a marriage to occur, as they have significant meaning in a traditional Hmong marriage ceremony. A list of essential traditional marriage artifacts is located in Appendix B. Cummings and Worley (2005) discussed the importance of the organization's culture and the elements of culture that help members of an organization "make sense out of their every day life in the organization" (p. 483). Those cultural elements are "artifacts, norms, values, and basic assumptions that are more or less shared by the organization member" (p. 483). Hmong also have cultural elements that help them understand and find meaning in their traditional practices. According to Cummings and Worley (2005):

> Artifacts are the highest level of cultural manifestations. These are the visible symbols of the deeper levels of culture, such as norms, values, and basic assumptions. They include observable behaviors of members, such as clothing and language; the structures, systems, procedures, and rules; and physical aspects of the organization, such as décor, space arrangements, and nose levels. (p. 484)

Regardless of the types of traditional marriage arrangements, the Hmong marriage ceremony rituals are extremely complex and are based on a structured, sequential procedure that is filled with rituals, marriage songs, and proverbs that are strictly followed. Hmong traditional marriage practices are based on sequential ceremonies along with a strict code of conduct that is governed by rules and specific rituals. Within these rituals, the Hmong's beliefs and values related to marriage and life are held. Special official marriage ceremonial names are given to the individuals in the official marriage party on both sides of the families, and these official names are used throughout the marriage ceremony rituals. Adherence to the strict rules of conduct is obeyed by both sides of the family throughout the marriage ceremony ritual.

A traditional Hmong marriage ceremony involves a multitude of people from both the groom's and the bride's sides of the family. Hmong marriage ceremonies exemplify the need for Hmong to live in clusters because any decision that was made involved the entire kinship or *kwv tij*. Oftentimes, decisions are made by soliciting input and feedback from everyone in the kinship before coming to a consensus on a decision.

Depending on the type of marriage arrangement, the beginning of a marriage ceremony is slightly different; however, the central part of the marriage ceremony rituals is the same, with some slight variations according to the dialect of the bride. If the groom is Green Hmong and the bride is White Hmong, the marriage ceremony will be conducted according to the White Hmong's marriage ceremony rituals. Oftentimes the *mejkoob* must speak the dialect of the bride's parents as a respect for the bride's family and customs. In a marriage ceremony, the groom's marriage party has to follow the customs and rituals of the bride's family. The bride's family usually dictates the complexity or simplicity of the marriage ceremony rituals. Bertrais (1978) stated:

> In spite of the peculiarities of language, the most of which amount to some regular changes, the Green Hmong songs and the White Hmong songs are identical. Those of one group are perfectly understood by the people of the other. The composition of the songs is the same; there exists only a regular transference from one group to the other. The titles and the contents are the same for both the White and the Green Hmong series. Marriage between the two groups is rather frequent, each party bringing along its own go-betweens and other officials. (p. 4)

Journey to America

Although the Hmong may have sought temporary freedom from ruling governments in China, they came under another type of governmental rule in their new homeland in the 1800s. Laos was a part of the French colony, and the Hmong had to abide by the French government. In March 1945, French colonial rule ceased and Laos declared independence, and by 1955, Laos was fully recognized as an independent nation (Lee, 1982). Civil war broke out in Laos between the ruling government—the Royal Lao Government—and the Pathet Lao, which favored communism. In the 1960s, the Hmong were actively involved in the Royal Lao governmental affairs and military campaigns.

The United States Central Intelligence Agency (CIA) actively recruited and trained the Hmong as the CIA's "secret army." "In exchange for a promise of protection should the United States withdraw from their country, thousands of Hmong men were hired by the CIA to fight the Communist guerrillas—the Pathet Lao" (Cerhan, 1990, p. 89). They operated from the remote mountain ranges of northern Laos in Long Chieng. They pushed back the Communist guerrillas along the Ho Chi Minh Trail and rescued American pilots who were shot down in this area (Ng, 1995). It was estimated that as many as 100,000 Hmong perished during the 14-year war, while one third of the Hmong population was banished (Johnson & Yang, 1992). Robbins (1987) reported that there were so many Hmong casualties that toward the end of the war, there were only boys left fighting in the war.

In 1975, the United States withdrew from the war in Laos. The Pathet Lao had total control over Laos. Because of the Hmong's affiliation with the Royal Lao military and the United States, they were sentenced to extinction by the Pathet Lao government. Thousands of Hmong were forced to leave Laos and flee into refugee camps in Thailand (Cerhan, 1990; Lee,

1982). Cappelletty (1986) stated that "The Lao People's Democratic Republic (LPDR) was determined to 'rip the cancer out by the roots' and whole villages of Hmong were destroyed" (p. 28). To escape persecution, the Hmong escaped to Thailand by crossing the deep and treacherous Mekong River, which bordered Thailand and Laos (Ng, 1995).

The journey to the Mekong River was not easy, and many families had to travel from 30 to 300 miles before they reached the river's shore. On their way to the river, many people ran out of food, and they had to eat available roots, tree barks, and boiled leaves. Many infants and children died from opium overdoses, which were used to keep them from making noise and crying. Thousands of people died along the way from insect or snake bites, hunger, thirst, and ambush (Cappelletty, 1986).

When the Hmong reached the Thai camps, life was not any better. They often had to live in overcrowded houses, and sanitation was poor. Food distribution was measured by the number of family members in the household and the age of each member, which meant that smaller families barely made it through to the next food distribution (Ka Xiong, personal communication, December 31, 2007). Furthermore, Ka Xiong indicated that many Hmong had to trade what they could savage from crossing the Mekong River to purchase food in between food distributions. For others, they had to undergo hard labor in nearby Thai farmlands in exchange for food or low payments for their work.

In mid-1975, 14 voluntary agencies were funded by the U.S. federal government to expedite the process of resettling the Hmong refugees from Thailand to Western countries in collaboration with the Intergovernmental Committee for European Migration (ICEM; Lo, 2001). Lo indicated that "Vang Pao and many of the Hmong military leaders were among the first to enter the U.S. Over 45,000 Hmong were left for the next open slots" (p. 71). Starting in 1976, the Hmong started to arrive in the United States. In 1978, the researcher, along with her family, was sponsored by the International Rescue Committee (IRC) in

New York to come to the U.S., and the researcher's family arrived in New York City, New York, on July 28, 1978.

Although thousands of the Hmong resettled in countries such as Canada, France, Argentina, Australia, French-Guinea, Germany, and the United States of America, there were still some of the Hmong who did not wish to move to any of these countries. Instead, they chose to stay in the refugee camps of Thailand with the eventual hope of returning to Laos. Other Hmong decided to retreat back into the high mountains of Thailand and became Thai citizens. From 2004 to 2006, the United States accepted the last wave of Hmong refugees from Wat Tham Krabok in Thailand to the USA (Wang Fu Vang, personal communication, March 19, 2008).

Traditional Hmong Marriage Ceremony Rituals
as a Result of Resettlement

Upon arriving in the United States, the Immigration and Naturalization Service dispersed the Hmong throughout several states. However, because of their clan and family orientation, many of the Hmong still chose to live close together in huge numbers mainly in California, Minnesota, Wisconsin, and several other states. The Hmong can now be found in almost every one of the states in the United States (Bonner & Chang, 1995; Vang, 2008).

The Hmong have acclimatized to their new environments and have made some radical changes in the past 30 years since their arrival to the U.S. in the mid-1970s. When they first came, language barriers prevented them from obtaining any significant type of employment, and many of them depended on governmental assistance programs for their survival (Moua, 2006). Kou Yang (1997) stated that many of the older Hmong men were having trouble acculturating to the culture of this country due to language barriers and cultural differences. Oftentimes they had to rely on younger persons "for language translation and cultural interpretation" (Yang, 1997, p. 7). There was a great deal of generational conflicts among the young's acceptance and acculturation to the Western society while the older generation were continuing to maintain their traditional customs (Tatman, 2004).

Employment

However, after being in the U.S. for 30 years, the Hmong have aggressively been moving into the workforce in many different trades and professions, ranging from blue-collar jobs to white-collar employment, with a number of successful entrepreneurs in many types of businesses (Lee, 2005a, 2005b, 2005c, 2005d, 2005e; Moua, 2006; Vang, 2008). The median income for the Hmong in the 2000 Census was between $35,000 to $50,000 nationwide, and the number of homeowners was about 39% (Pfeifer & Lee, 2000). Additionally, the Hmong's acculturation to the American society was rapidly successful as evidenced by having Hmong individuals who were found in influential political positions, including a state senator, state representative, city council, and school board members.

Education

Education is another area where the Hmong are making "extraordinary strides, especially considering that they mostly came as illiterate refugees from a tribal, shifting agricultural, and hunter-gatherer society. They are now predominantly employed, have attended some school, and can speak some English" (Westermeyer, Neider, & Callies, 1989, p. 138). In fact, the number of Hmong individuals in universities was slightly over 30 in the early 1970s in Laos (Vang, 2008). Interestingly, now there are about 27.2% of Hmong graduates from high school, 11.7% had associate's or bachelor's degrees, and 1.5% had earned graduate degrees (Pfeifer & Yang, 2000). Comparing these percentages to where they were 30 years ago, it appears the Hmong have made significant gains in educational achievements.

Gender Roles

Relative to gender and roles, the Hmong have experienced a significant paradigm shift. Traditionally, gender and generation status served as stature and power in the Hmong family and clan. Elder men had more power in making decisions than did women and young adults. However, Vang (2008) stated that there has been a shift in the Hmong social system as the younger generation of Hmong men and women are moving into leadership roles in today's society. Dana (1993) also indicated that women and men are now more equal partners in making decisions and supporting the family. Women are now working outside of the home and also becoming breadwinners instead of relying on their husbands to provide for the family (Tatman, 2004).

Clan Cohesiveness

Despite being dispersed throughout the U.S. when they first arrived, the Hmong's clan and kinship system has remained intact (Vang, 2008), as the Hmong have migrated back to areas to be with their relatives and clans who were located there (Dana, 1993). Additionally, Lo (2001) stated that the Hmong continue to utilize traditional ways of resolving conflicts through the support of their clan system.

Marriage Ceremony Options

Traditional Hmong marriage ceremonies have continued to be practiced among the Hmong throughout the USA; however, some young couples may choose to have two different types of marriage ceremonies. One is the traditional Hmong marriage ceremony out of respect for their parents and to suffice the legitimacy of a marriage according to traditional Hmong customs and traditions, and the other is an *American wedding*, which mirrors the American marriage institution of this country (Keown-Bomar, 2004). Mua (2002) concurred that since 1975, more Hmong have been converted to Christianity and because of this change in religion, there has been more integration of the Hmong marriage traditions with Christianity, which is more reflective of the demands in this new society than ever before. With more of the Hmong embracing Christianity, Christian-type marriage ceremonies are becoming more prominent, especially among those Hmong who are church members in their new communities. However, even though some Hmong have converted to Christianity, they still value and continue to practice their traditional Hmong marriage ceremonies (Lo, 2001).

Hmong New Year

Evidence of the adaptations and accommodations for change for the Hmong is most noticeable during Hmong New Year's celebrations. Many of the young men and women no longer wear Hmong traditional costumes or play *pov pob* or tossing ball. Only a few of the Hmong know how to sing their traditional folk songs, and they have adopted new practices during the Hmong New Year, including beauty pageants, music and dance competitions, sports events, and they invite a large number of product and service-based vendors to join in the celebration (Vang, 2008).

Decision-Making Dynamics

The Hmong's traditional value of collectivism and communal decision making is now much more individualistic and self-centered among some of the younger Hmong generations. Mua (2002) stated that in terms of marriage, Hmong youths are making decisions based on personal choice rather than the more traditional communal decisions. By adapting to mainstream American culture, some Hmong youths are transitioning from traditional values of the community-based decisions to ones with more individualistic influence. Meredith and Rowe (1986a, 1986b) stated that many of the Hmong felt that the young adults should have some choice in making the decision on who they wanted to marry.

Acculturation and Assimilation

Through acculturation and assimilation, the Hmong have adapted to the different environments and cultures of the U.S. Morgan (1997) indicated that an organism has to adapt to its new environment in order to survive. The Hmong have transitioned from their resettlement in the U.S. to becoming more acculturated into the American society during the last 30 years in order to be competitive. Although one of the essential fabrics of the Hmong culture is that of marriage traditions and rituals, the American culture has influenced this unique and complex tradition to one that is slowly reflecting the traditions of this country.

By viewing the traditional Hmong marriage ceremony from the standpoint of an institution, the Hmong marriage ceremony institution is now beginning to merge into the *American wedding* institution. When two institutions are merged, modifications and accommodations are frequently made, perhaps even downsizing, to create a more meaningful-based and integrated institution. If this is the case of the traditional Hmong marriage ceremony as it morphs to that of the American wedding, then perhaps the Hmong in the USA have changed their marriage ceremony institution to conform to the rituals and customs of the culture of this country.

Hmong Marriage Ceremonial Rituals
in the USA

To provide an illustration of some of the changes in the traditional Hmong marriage ceremonies and rituals in the U.S., a descriptive story of a recent marriage ceremony follows to highlight some of those changes. John and Mai Tong were both born and raised in Fresno, California, and this is their marriage story.

It was in the fall of 1997 when John Moua and May Tong Vang met in their zoology class at California State University, Fresno. They were told that throughout this course, they had to select a partner for labs and study sessions. Because they happened to sit next to each other in the class, they decided that it would be easy to just partner together, since they did not know anyone else in the class. This engagement was the beginning of a journey that would eventually lead them to love, marriage, and parenthood.

After dating for 2 years, John graduated from college and obtained a full-time job while May Tong still had a year left in her studies before completion of her degree. John had been saving money to pay for May Tong's engagement ring and for their marriage ceremonies ever since he started working.

Eventually, May Tong was finished with school in 2000, and John proposed to her that summer. Although they did not do a formal engagement party nor let their parents formally know that they were engaged, May Tong wore the engagement ring proudly on her ring finger. They both decided that they wanted to marry in the spring when life seems to be renewed for all forms of living things. Although their parents were not aware of their plans, they had already begun preparing for their *American wedding* ceremony by reserving halls and making plans for what would be needed. They decided that they would have their American wedding on Sunday, April 15, 2001.

Based on the American wedding date, John and May Tong had to plan their Hmong traditional marriage ceremony as close to this date as possible in order to have both of their marriage celebrations completed within a week of each other. Therefore, in the early days of April 2001, John informed his parents that he would be marrying May Tong within the next couple of days and, in essence, was asking for his parents' approval of the marriage. Since John's parents had met and had a chance to know May Tong well in the years that they had been dating, John's parents were happy and relieved to know that their son would be married to a good person.

A couple of days later, John asked May Tong to marry him by going with him to his parents' home. Although nervous and yet happy, May tong agreed to go with John to his home. Upon arriving at John's home, his parents welcomed May Tong to the family with a live chicken in hand, making three circles over May Tong's head. After that, John and May Tong were asked to sit and join their family to converse about their wedding plans.

May Tong noticed that there were a couple of male adults in the living room joining them in the conversations regarding their marriage ceremonies. May Tong also noticed that they had cigarette packs in hand while John and his father counted several hundreds of dollars in their presence. Shortly after that, these individuals left. John told May Tong that these informants were heading to May Tong's parents' home to inform them of the elopement.

When the informants arrived at May Tong's home, May Tong's parents were surprised to hear that May Tong had gotten married. Although sad they knew that their daughter was ready for marriage, and it was just a matter of time before she and John would marry each other. May Tong's parents accepted the cigarettes and the money from the informants. The informants told May Tong's parents that they were only informing them of the marriage, but that the marriage ceremonies would be a conversation between their children and the two sets of parents.

A meal was prepared for John's family and relatives prior to their departure to May Tong's home on that Friday morning. John's best friend, Jeff, would be his best man; his cousin, Xiong, would be the *aub nraa*; and John's niece, Madisen, would be a bridesmaid for May Tong. Tong Pao would be the *mejkoob*, or go-between, for John's side of the family. After John and Jeff kneeled and bowed to all of John's ancestors, parents, uncles, aunts, and relatives, they left to go to May Tong's home. Because they needed to eat the lunch in between the two houses and there were not any small parks nearby to stop for lunch, they decided to eat outside of John's house. Tong Pao offered some chicken and rice to the spirit in that area and then proceeded to finish the meal with the rest of the marriage party.

When they arrived at May Tong's home, May Tong's parents greeted them all warmly and invited them into their home. Although May Tong's parents asked them all to sit, only May Tong, Madisen, and Xiong sat while John and Jeff kneeled and bowed to May Tong's parents, aunts, uncles, and the prosperity spirit along with the house spirits.

After that Tong Pao took the Marriage Umbrella to where the prosperity spirit paper was and put it down on the floor with the top pointing up. From there, a table was set in the living room for the marriage negotiation between the go-betweens. After 4 hours of negotiation, a bride price of $5,000 with an additional $800 for the celebration expense was agreed upon by both sides. Since May Tong was the older of the two daughters, permission was not needed from her younger sister for the marriage. Additionally, although John and May Tong had been dating for the past 3½ years, they had been most respectful and cordial in their interactions at May Tong's home and among May Tong's family and so no penalty prize was charged to John. May Tong's parents said that they wanted the Hmong traditional marriage ceremony to be simple so that everyone would be rested and prepared for the American wedding on Sunday. They closed the marriage negotiation around 9:00 P.M. and so the discussions among May Tong, John, and the rest of the marriage party members and families now revolved around the excitement of the American wedding.

The next morning, May Tong's brother and cousins went to the slaughterhouse and got a pig for the main feast of the Hmong marriage ceremony. John and Jeff helped May Tong's relatives with chopping the meat while May Tong and Madisen helped with the preparation of the salad and vegetables. Around noon the food was ready and everyone who was invited to the marriage ceremony enjoyed a festive meal.   After the meal, everything was cleared from the table and the set-up for the marriage ceremony rituals began. The bride's *mejkoob* invited all the main participants to come and sit at their assigned chairs around the table. At this time, the master of ceremony discussed with the two *mejkoob* the process of the marriage ceremony rituals. Traditionally, there were many rounds of alcoholic drinks during the ceremony, but the master of ceremony and May Tong's parents wanted only six rounds of drinks. The master of ceremony was really relaxed with the choice of drinks throughout this ceremony, and participants were given the choice of soft drinks, water, or beer. The rituals that the master of ceremony followed were the *qab suav yaig* or the omen chicken, *cawv poob plaag* or recognition of the bride's parents and relatives, *laig dlaab tshoob* or offerings to the marriage spirit. After that, Tong Pao told John to hold May Tong's hand and walk out of May Tong's parents' home. When all of the marriage party had left, Tong Pao tore the special *separation chicken* in half and gave the half without the head to May Tong's *mejkoob* while he took the side with the head for May Tong.

When they arrived at John's home, they had lunch on their front porch. Again, Tong Pao offered a little rice and chicken to the spirit of the area. After a short ritual at the door, they were welcomed back home. A table was already set and the marriage party members were asked to take their places on the chairs around the table. Tong Pao shared with John's family the smoothness of the marriage ceremony celebration at May Tong's home. He also read the list of gifts and monies given to May Tong and John by May Tong's parents and relatives. After that, each member of the marriage party was thanked by Johns' relatives. A couple of the elders, including Tong Pao, blessed May Tong and John for a long life filled with many children, happiness, and good fortune. At the end of the ritual, John stood next to his father and thanked their relatives for their help in John's traditional Hmong marriage ceremony. They then invited everyone to join John and May Tong's American wedding the next day at a nearby hall.

The next day, May Tong and John's American wedding went according to plan. They had packed the night before for their honeymoon departure later on that evening to Hawaii. As they looked out the window of the airplane to the blue lagoons of the islands, they both took deep breaths and closed their eyes. They knew that the rest of their life together was yet to be unfolded; what they held onto was how fate had brought them together and that destiny would be theirs to make happily-ever-after a lifetime of memorable moments.

In the previous example, the Hmong traditional marriage ceremonies in the U.S. were compressed into 1 day and a half with the bridegroom going to the bride's home on a Friday afternoon and then returning home on Saturday late afternoon. Many couples may have an additional American wedding, which may lead into another day, but it would not be an extension of the traditional Hmong marriage ceremony rituals.

Summary

The Hmong have a long history of relocating from one region to another in search of finding a better land to grow crops and raise a family. According to Quincy (1988), the Hmong may have been one of the immigrant groups who journeyed from Siberia to the Manchuria region of China in early 2500 B.C. and then slowly migrated southward to Southern China beyond Yangtze and the Yellow Rivers (Lie-Young, Yang, Rai, & Vang, 2004). Eventually they went beyond the borders of China into northern Vietnam and then finally to Laos in the early 1800s (Quincy, 1988). In Laos the Hmong thrived on the rich terrains of the mountainous regions of Xieng Khoung to cultivate farmlands using the slash-and-burn methods and lived in small villages amongst the hilltops away from the lowland Laotians and other minority groups in the region (Pfaff, 1995). By maintaining their solidarity from the rest of the groups in the region, the Hmong lived in peace and harmony, practicing their traditional ways of life without interference from outsiders.

The Hmong have preserved their way of life for thousands of years. In Laos, they continued to practice their traditional customs and rituals. One of the traditional Hmong cornerstone practices is their traditional marriage ceremony rituals. The Hmong have a unique marriage ceremony ritual with complex rules, etiquette, elements, and essential roles for all participants involved. There was a great deal of respect and humbleness within the Hmong community while observing this ritual among the families who celebrated this tradition.

However, in the early 1960s, the Hmong were recruited by the U.S. Central Intelligence Agency (CIA) to be trained as guerilla fighters in rescuing downed U.S. pilots and defending against the North Vietnamese and Pathet Lao divisions (Dao, 1982; Vang, 2008). General Vang Pao was air lifted out of Laos since "the left's influence was gaining momentum and those who had allied with foreigners and had a higher military rank would be viewed as a threat to the new regime," thousands of Hmong left Laos to go to Thailand in fear of persecution (Vang, 2008, p. 6). The Hmong were granted temporary refuge in the refugee camps of Thailand while they waited for host countries to sponsor them for resettlement. A large wave of the Hmong were allowed to resettle in the United States, Canada, Argentina, Australia, France, Germany, and French-Guinea beginning in June of 1976 "When the U.S. Congress passed the Indochina Migration and Refugee Assistance Act in May 1975" (Vang, 2008, p. 10).

In the U.S., there was a "scattering policy" employed in order to disperse the Hmong refugees evenly throughout the chosen urban communities where resettlement would take place (Dana, 1993, p. 10). Many of the Hmong migrated and concentrated in areas of California, Minnesota, and Wisconsin for reunification with clans and other related kin (Dana, 1993; Vang, 2008).

Since the Hmong's first arrival in the U.S., they have continuously attempted to adapt to and assimilate into the American society and culture. By viewing the Hmong as an institution, they have gone through the three phases of transition as described by Bridges (2003) as they acculturated and assimilated into their new society. When the Hmong first arrived in the U.S., they experienced loss, hopelessness, fear, isolation, and uncertainty of the future (Hayes, 1987; Yang, 1997). Fong (2004a, 2004b) indicated that when a group of people left their home country to go to another one, they should not leave behind their cultural values in the process.

Slowly, the Hmong have moved into Bridge's neutral zone where they were in a state of uncertainty, understanding that they would need to adjust to the U.S. society quickly in order to survive and yet were still clinging to the comforts of the past. Some elders, especially those in the veteran and some baby boomer generations, still had hopes of one day returning to Laos (Yang, 1997). However, the majority of the Hmong had started to enroll in English classes and were taking technical courses at training facilities or vocational schools to learn new trades and skills. Although some Hmong were having difficulty adjusting and adapting to the life of this country, many of them were preparing themselves to become productive citizens in the new homeland. Although some individuals and perhaps some groups of the Hmong may have oscillated back and forth between this neutral zone phase and the next phase at their own pace, there were many of the Hmong who were moving into the final phase of their new beginning.

In the new beginning, the Hmong were rapidly making radical changes in many areas of their lives since resettlement in the U.S. Moua (2006) stated that in the 1990s there were many successful Hmong business people, professors, lawyers, educators, and multimillionaires, while a handful of the Hmong had attained influential roles as a state senator, state representative, city councilmen, and school board members. In Bridge's (2003) new beginning phase, the Hmong had certainly moved forward with the opportunities that were available for them in the U.S.

The Hmong have the capability to adapt and change as an institution within the demands of their new environment, and yet they have managed to preserve their fundamental foundations, which are rooted in traditional customs and rituals (Newman & Nollen, 1998). Vang (2008) stated that "Contrary to popular perception, Hmong culture has not been static, but, rather, flexible and evolving. Migration . . . has inspired tremendous changes in the ways traditions are carried out" (p. 39). "Regardless of where they reside, Hmong have preserved some aspects of their culture and its traditions at the same time they have accepted new cultural expressions—not unlike other immigrant groups in America" (p. 49). As the Hmong assimilate and acculturate into the U.S. society, their traditional marriage ceremony rituals will be modified and continue to change in order to align themselves with the mainstream U.S. culture and customs.

Chapter 3

METHODOLOGY

This chapter begins with a brief discussion on using qualitative research as the methodology for discovering and understanding the factors that affected the changes in traditional Hmong marriage ceremony practices. The remainder of the chapter focuses on the scope of the study, participant selection criteria, delimitations and assumptions, data collection and storage, and the qualitative data analysis process.

The method that typically is used for the collection of data for research projects depends on the type of study and the kind of data that are to be collected. In this project, the researcher conducted a qualitative research study to gain knowledge of the factors that influenced the Hmong to make changes and modifications to their traditional marriage ceremony practices. Taylor, Bogdan, and Walker (2000) reported that qualitative research is "concerned with the meanings people attach to things in their lives . . . [and] studies people in the context of their pasts and the situations in which they find themselves" (p. 490). "It is systematic research conducted with demanding, although not necessarily standardized, procedures" (p. 491). Ruona (2005) indicated, "Qualitative data deal with meanings . . . [and] thus data in the form of words. These words are derived from observations, interviews, or documents" (p. 234). She further stated, "participants' words represent their social realities. The primary charge during qualitative research is to capture, understand, and represent participants' perceptions and meanings through and in their own words" (p. 234).

To obtain the qualitative data for this study, the researcher conducted face-to-face in-depth interviews with individual participants residing in Fresno County and telephone interviews with participants who were located elsewhere. This method of interviewing was chosen to allow the researcher more opportunities to ask essential questions as well as to utilize more probing questions to obtain complete and thorough responses from the participants (Berg, 2007). When a participant was uncertain about the question, the researcher was able to clarify or rephrase the question for more clarity.

Scope of the Study

The scope of this study was based on the responses of the participants who were located in both California and Utah. The participants were specifically selected as a reliable source of knowledge in representing the 0.5-generation Hmong with different backgrounds in education, age, and religious beliefs. The responses from these participants were used to gain knowledge and further understand the factors that influenced the Hmong to change their traditional marriage ceremony practices in the U.S.

Participant Selection Criteria

The researcher gathered data from a purposive sample of the Hmong population (Berg, 2007). Although all of the Hmong who were residing in the United States could have been potential participants, the focus of this study was the 0.5 generation of Hmong males and females. This generation is composed of mostly generation Xers (Strauss & Howe, 1991; Zemke, Raines, & Filipczak, 2000). Generation Xer refers to someone who was born between 1961 and 1981 and currently between the ages of 25 to 45 years old (Zemke et al., 2000). Moua (2006) indicated that this generation "speaks, understands, reads, and writes RPA—Hmong, Thai, Laotian, and English" (p. 41). He further stated that this generation was able to understand the different cultures of the Hmong, Laotian, Thai, and American, which could be the key to Hmong's success in the U.S. The researcher was particularly interested in studying this generation who was between the ages of 35 to 45, and those aged 50 because these individuals were born in Laos and raised in the U.S. and have a comprehensive understanding and knowledge of both the U.S. and the Hmong culture.

Additionally, the participants in this study needed to have been born in Laos. Having lived first in Laos and then subsequently in the refugee camps of Thailand provided this group of people a common transitional stage when entering the United States. Being fluent in Hmong was a communication vehicle for being able to articulate changes in the traditional Hmong marriage ceremony rituals, and this particular group of Hmong was knowledgeable and solidly grounded in the traditional Hmong marriage ceremony rituals. Another important criterion for the participants was that they had been educated in the United States. In particular, these participants were chosen because they had obtained a high school diploma or college degree as evidence that they had some knowledge of the culture of what was now their home. This group of participants would most likely be able to provide their perspectives about the factors that were affecting the traditional Hmong marriage ceremony as a result of living in the United States.

The number of participants required for this study was dependent on the eventual saturation point that would be reached with data that were being collected. Fendya (1995) indicated that when the information was adequate for the purpose and the goals of the phenomenon being studied, then saturation would be achieved. Although the number of participants was not specified, Fendya stated that collecting data from between 5 to 10 participants may be adequate fo the purpose of the research. In presenting the results in Chapter 4, the names of the participants in this study have been changed to protect the confidentiality of the participants.

Data Collection

The researcher contacted Hmong friends and colleagues for potential research participants who would meet the criteria that were desired for this study. Upon obtaining the names of potential individual participants, the researcher made personal telephone calls to them. Once the participant volunteered to take part in this study, a convenient date, time, and location were arranged for the interview process.

The interviews were conducted by the researcher in both the Hmong and English languages. The interviews took place where the participants decided they were most comfortable and would have few distractions. Several interviews took place at the participants' homes while others took place at the participants' workplace, researcher's home, and at a quiet location inside of a restaurant. Telephone interviews were conducted from the participants' homes.

The interviewing process began with the researcher greeting the participant and having a brief conversation with the participant to establish a relationship and to make the participant feel more comfortable with the process. Customarily, the Hmong begin a conversation about some unrelated topics to establish rapport and trust before redirecting the discussion to the issues at hand. The researcher observed similar cultural conversational etiquette when conducting the interviews with the selected participants.

After the researcher felt that the participant was fairly comfortable with the interview process, the researcher thanked the participant for agreeing to be interviewed for this study. The researcher then explained the purpose of the study and the interview procedure. In addition, the researcher shared how the data would be stored and subsequently destroyed after the completion of the study. The researcher also explained how the data would be transcribed to secure confidentiality for the participant if the participant agreed to have the interview audiotaped by the researcher. If the participant did not agree to have the interview audiotaped, the researcher informed the participant about the need for the researcher to take notes throughout the interview as a way to record the information that the participant was providing.

If the participant agreed with the procedures up to this point, the researcher began reading the Introduction to the Participant Statement (Appendix C) and had the participant sign a consent form (Appendix D) prior to starting the interview. Again, the researcher informed the participant that the interview would be audiotaped so that the data could be transcribed or, if the participant had not agreed to be audiotaped, the participant was reminded that the researcher would be taking notes.

The participant was asked to complete a demographic questionnaire (Appendix E), which consisted of 10 questions. After the participant completed the demographic questionnaire, the researcher began the open-ended questions related to the traditional Hmong marriage ceremony rituals. At the end of each interview, the researcher asked the participant for additional follow-up interviews in case clarifications were needed regarding the information that he or she had provided. After the interviews were conducted and the data were transcribed, it was not necessary to have any follow-up interview.

Research Questions

The questions for this study were constructed to capture answers for the research question that focused on identifying the factors that were related to the 0.5-generation Hmong in making changes in their traditional Hmong marriage ceremony rituals. From a broad perspective, the questions were designed to learn about the participants' perceptions of the traditional Hmong marriage ceremony rituals that were being practiced by their generation as well as the future Hmong generations who were living in the United States. The semistructured interview questions (Appendix F) were based on the following questions, which guided this study:

    1. Are the Hmong in this country still practicing the traditional marriage ceremony rituals?

    2. Do they follow the same traditional Hmong marriage ceremony rituals? What does the modification of the Hmong marriage ceremony rituals look like?

    3. What are some of the factors that cause the Hmong to change their traditional marriage ceremony rituals in the United States?

Delimitations and Assumptions

    The focused population for this study was the 0.5-generation Hmong in the United States, and the participants were primarily located in Fresno County in California and the state of Utah. The data were collected in February and March of 2008, and reflected a limited number of participants. Hmong marriage values from other regions of the United States were not taken into consideration for this study. Since the 0.5-generation Hmong was considered to be a bridge between the older Hmong generation and the younger generations who are currently residing in the United States, they were specifically chosen for this study to learn more about their beliefs of the traditional marriage rituals.

Data Storage

    The participant's name for these interviews only appeared on the consent form that was signed prior to the interviews. The consent form and the participant's response to the questions were not associated in any way. Each participant was assigned a numeric number for the purpose of identification. To further secure confidentiality for the participants, the recorded audiotapes were assigned a number corresponding to the same numeric number as the transcribed data. The audiotapes were kept until the information was transcribed, then were erased and subsequently destroyed. To prevent any association of the informed consent form with the recorded audiotapes, the documents were stored in separate locked file cabinets in a locked room at the researcher's residence.

Qualitative Data Analysis Procedure

The methodology approach used for interpreting and drawing meanings from the collected qualitative data was thematic analysis (Taylor & Bogdan, 1984). This approach was chosen to discover themes and patterns to answer the research question. Although the research question for this study was focused on discovering and understanding the factors that affect the traditional Hmong marriage ceremony rituals and practices, there were several guided questions that provided rich and valuable information about the 0.5-generation Hmong and perhaps the direction of future Hmong marriages in the United States. The following was the process used for analyzing the data in this study.

Upon the completion of each interview, the researcher transcribed the data from the audiotape. After all the interviews were transcribed, the responses were separated and grouped according to the interview questions. In reading through the responses for each question, the researcher read and reread the responses looking for emerging themes and patterns and underlying similarities (Taylor & Bogdan, 1984). Taylor and Bogdan indicated the need to "search through your data for emerging themes or patterns" (p. 13). As themes and patterns were identified, thematic categories were formed, and names that appropriately fit the categories were developed. According to Creswell (2002), this process includes "segmenting sentences or paragraphs into categories, and labeling those categories with a term" (p. 192). Each theme category was given a single word name or a phrase. This process was used for all the responses to each interview question. As a result, each question had several thematic categories.

Once the thematic categories were named, the participants' transcribed responses were sorted and placed into the most appropriate category. This process was used for all of the responses and questions with the exception of some of the data that did not fit into any of the existing categories and for Interview Question 1.

For Question 1, the researcher focused on obtaining information about the participant's knowledge of the traditional Hmong marriage ceremony rituals. The participants' responses were tallied into three categories based on the number of rituals that the participants indicated that they knew relative to the elements of traditional Hmong marriage ceremony rituals and practices.

Questions 2, 4, and 5 were guided questions to obtain more information about the practice of the traditional Hmong marriage ceremony rituals in the U.S. There were some inconsistencies with the participants' responses for these questions. Because of some of the participants' responses to the semistructured interview questions, there was some difficulty in categorizing the information so it could be coded and themed.

The participants' responses to Interview Question 3 directly answer the research question on discovering the factors that affected the traditional Hmong marriage ceremony. Each of the participants' responses was tagged and sorted according to where the responses best fit in the thematic categories. There were several responses that did not fit into any of the categories; however, they were also reported in the Results chapter because they represented some factors that have significant bearings on the research question. The categories for this particular question were further sorted to analyze meaningful text. In addition to drawing conclusions from the themed categories, the researcher also utilized quotes from meaningful text in the participants' responses to learning about the significant changes to traditional Hmong marriage ceremony rituals that had occurred after the resettlement in the U.S.

Summary

The research methodology that was utilized for this study was qualitative in nature. This study was conducted to discover and understand significant factors that were affecting changes in the traditional Hmong marriage ceremony through a process of categorizing recurrent themes from the participants' responses from a semistructured interview.

The participants who were selected for this study were the 0.5-generation Hmong between the ages of 35 and 50 and were especially chosen because they were grounded in the traditional Hmong cultures as well as the mainstream American culture. These participants were able to provide vital information about the factors that had affected Hmong individuals as a cultural group who had chosen to make changes in their traditional Hmong marriage ceremonies as they began to settle in their new American home 30 years ago. The individuals in this study were exclusive to the Hmong who were living in California and Utah. Although all of the 0.5-generation Hmong residing within the U.S. could have been potential participants in this study, the researcher chose the individual participants in these particular states for the sample.

Thematic analysis was the methodology chosen for analyzing the data in this study. The participants' responses were organized according to "data-driven codes" for themes and patterns (Ruona, 2005, p. 242). The themes were then categorized and appropriate words or phrases were assigned to each category. Based on the designated categories, meaningful texts were extracted and conclusions were drawn.

Chapter 4

RESULTS

This chapter discusses the results obtained from the 12 participants, which were taken from the data in the semistructured interview process. The first half of this chapter summarizes the themes of each of the questions, while the second half of the chapter presents the factors that resulted in changes related to the research question and possible future modifications in the younger Hmong generations' marriage ceremony rituals. The names used in presenting the results throughout this chapter are fictitious to protect the confidentiality of the participants.

Responses to Demographic Questions

The participants for this study were composed of 7 males and 5 females with an age range from 35 to 49 years old. All of the participants resided in the states of California and Utah. All of the participants have at some time lived in Fresno, California, prior to moving to other cities in California and Utah.

The time span for the participants' arrival in the U.S. began in 1976, and continued through 1983, and they have lived in the U.S. for 25 to 32 years. The age of these participants upon arrival in the U.S. was from 4 to 21 years of age. Most of them began their schooling in the USA at the primary grade levels, while several started in high school and 1 at the adult school level. There were 2 high school graduates, 1 earned a high school diploma along with a vocational training certificate, 2 held associate of arts degrees, 2 obtained bachelor's degrees, and 5 had master's degrees.

All of the participants were married and had children. They all spoke fluent Hmong as well as English. Six of the participants practiced the traditional Hmong religion of Animism and Ancestral Worship, and 6 of them had converted to Christianity.

Knowledge of the Traditional Hmong
Marriage Ceremony Rituals

Table 1 illustrates the number of participants who responded to Question 1 regarding their knowledge of the traditional Hmong marriage ceremony rituals. Five of the participants stated that they knew most of the traditional

Table 1
Knowledge of Traditional Marriage Ceremony Rituals*

Participants know 1-2 rituals	Participants know 3-4 rituals	Participants know 5 or more rituals
4	3	5

*Based on 10 traditional Hmong marriage ceremony rituals.

Hmong marriage ceremony rituals. Three of them indicated that they knew some of the rituals, but not all of the details of the marriage rituals. Four of the participants knew one or two of the apparent rituals, such as the *lwm qab*, which is the ritual of using a live chicken circling over the bride's head to welcome her soul to the groom's family or the *hu plig*, which is the soul calling ritual of the bride.

Question 2 asked the participants about their thoughts and feelings related to the traditional Hmong marriage ceremony rituals. There was a wide range of responses to this question, with some of the participants stating that they felt the traditional Hmong marriage ceremony rituals were important because they connected and would bind the families and clans together who were involved in the marriage. Cheng stated:

> I think it makes a lot of sense. It's important. Back in the old country, it's almost like a ritual that ties the whole family together. It's a way of having the two families connect together. Back in Laos, it's a celebration where the whole village come to listen and participate.

Similarly, Maly stated:

> I feel very strong about it. I feel bad that the younger generations don't feel the same about it. For me as a bride, I feel I am more valued and people just can't say what they want to say without paying a price for it. My parents, my family, all gain an extended family.

They also indicated that the rituals provided opportunities for relatives to bless and advise the couple on the ways of a married life as they were preparing to start their new lives together. Nhia reminisced about wanting to experience a full Hmong marriage ceremony:

> I feel that it's important. I mean looking back we didn't do everything and I wish we had. I know that we hadn't done it made me wish we had. We had a Hmong wedding but we didn't have a true Hmong wedding.

Some of the participants stated that the Hmong in this generation and the younger generations are moving away from the traditional marriage ceremony rituals. They indicated that there was a need to maintain the ceremony rituals since the Hmong

will continue to practice these rituals for perhaps the next 50 years. Tong emphasized the need to learn the traditional rituals:
> Even though we don't know the rituals, there are still some that are learning them. Though we don't know, we are Hmong and so we still have to keep up with the rituals. Just like me, I don't know a lot about the rituals even though my father knows a lot.

Neng emphasized that the Hmong were most likely losing their culture and traditions. She stated, "I feel that it's good that we're continuing our traditional rituals to keep it going, but not a lot of people know them and so we're losing the culture." There was a great deal of concern expressed by some of the participants that by not practicing the traditional rituals, in the future the Hmong might only be reading documented rituals rather than actively practicing them.

Some of the participants reported that maintaining the rituals was important, but there should be some consideration given to eliminating some of the rituals in order to condense the length of the ceremony. A couple of the participant said that there should be fewer individuals involved in the ceremonial rituals. They also stated that the parents on both the bride's and the groom's side should negotiate the marriage ceremony among themselves without involving any relatives, *mejkoob* or go-between persons. Toua indicated the need to adjust the rituals to the environment: "Due to the environment and situation here in the USA, I think we should eliminate some of the unnecessary items. Even though these rituals are tradition, we will need to adjust to move forward with the environment and society."

However, some of the participants did not like the traditional Hmong marriage rituals at all. They felt that Hmong marriage rituals were a way of making money, since they used riddles and tests to trick the groom's party into making errors and then would penalize them for their mistakes with money and alcohol. This has caused conflicts among clans and families for future marriages. Additionally, 1 of the participants felt that the conflict of spiritual beliefs could be a potential cause for trouble during the negotiation of the marriage.

Based on the variety of views that were expressed regarding the traditional Hmong marriage ceremony rituals, there was not any consistency or common theme in these responses. These viewpoints indicated that the Hmong are still in a state of adapting and accommodating the old with the new, and it will probably take some time before there is more commonality of thoughts and opinions.

Modifications of the Traditional Hmong
Marriage Ceremony Rituals

The 0.5-generation Hmong is considered to be the generation that has connected the older generation to the younger generations by modifying the traditional rituals in response to the demands of the culture and the Hmong youths who are now residing in this country. When individuals in this particular generation were married, their marriage ceremonies encompassed many different forms, ranging from the traditional Hmong marriage ceremonies to the Americanized type of weddings. Of the 12 participants in this study, 6 individuals had followed all of the traditional Hmong marriage ceremony rituals, while 2 individuals' marriage ceremony rituals had been modified using only the most essential and basic of the rituals. Three of the 12 participants indicate that they had both a traditional Hmong marriage ceremony and an American wedding. One of the participants married someone with a different ethnic background but still chose to practice several of the selective Hmong marriage rituals during the marriage ceremony. One of the participants whose marriage ceremony was modified explained:

> We did the traditional Hmong marriage ceremony, but we skipped a lot of the traditional rituals also. We did not have a lot of the marriage songs, probably three to

four songs. Due to health concerns, we did not drink alcohol; we only drank soda. We did not drink the big alcohol drink at all, we only drank four or five rounds. It only took us 4 to 5 hours and we were done compared to some other ones that took over night. We did not have a lot of alcohol, because we do not want to make people sick from drinking too much. During the acquaintance ritual, only one of the brothers from my wife's family gave me a drink. Only one was allowed to *zeem* or acquaint the groom. Though they introduced themselves to me, the *mejkoob* did not allow alcohol. I did not go through a traumatic experience like others who got so drunk that they have to have a [another person to take the groom's place because he was too drunk] replacement.

Since there have been some mixed racial marriages among the Hmong, the Hmong parents have been receptive to change and have provided alternative options for the marriage ceremony. Nhia shared her marriage experience:

My parents had a hard time in terms of how we were going to do this. I mean, he is White and I'm Hmong. [Since the bride is Hmong] we had our own cultural way of running a marriage and so we decided to do it the Hmong way. Of course, we did not do everything the same way but as far as coming over and paying the dowry to my parents and the food, we did it the same way. We did not have a *mejkoob*, but our Hmong [clan] they came and did a little blessing, *hu plig* with a chicken, *khiteg* (with strings on the wrists ritual), *noj mov* (had a feast), giving gifts, I got some lecture. We did all the bargaining with the night before. They just say this is it. Whatever my parents wanted, they got. My parents knew that he was not Hmong and so they ask for $5,000 for me and then another $1,500 for food and that was it.

We didn't do an American wedding, we just went downtown. We already had a community wedding the Hmong way. It's important to make sure that it's legal in the American eyes.

Toua expanded on some of the modifications that were made during his traditional Hmong marriage ceremony:

I have seen some changes depending on the respective groups of Hmong people. Some of the changes include not using the chicken to *hu plig*, no kneel for some of the Hmong groups, no alcohol involvement. Some of the changes, I believe are positive moving forward.

Factors Influencing Changes in the Traditional Hmong Marriage Ceremony Rituals

Based on the participants' responses to the interview questions, there were some common themes that seemed to have influenced change in the Hmong's traditional marriage ceremony rituals since resettlement in the U.S. Some of the common themes that surfaced among the participants regarding the factors that resulted in changes to the traditional Hmong marriage ceremony rituals were: (a) time, (b) lack of knowledge of the rituals, (c) religion, (d) significance of rituals, (e) assimilation and acculturation to the American culture, (f) education, (g) mixed race marriages, (h) money, (in) language, and (j) shift in thinking from collectivism to individualism. The Hmong have begun to simplify their marriage ceremonies as a result of the above factors, and many have stopped practicing the rituals all together or have had their marriage ceremonies both the Hmong and the American way.

Time

One of the factors that the participants indicated regarding change to the traditional Hmong marriage ritual was a time factor. Because most individuals had to work during the weekdays, it was difficult for marriage ceremonies to be spread over multiple days as was done in Laos. Maly stated,

> I remember my parents telling me that some marriage proposals in Laos could last up to a week, if no agreement is made. I am glad this isn't happening here, as we all have to work, go to school, daily activities.

Neng agreed that time was a constraint for marriage ceremonies to be followed exactly in the traditional manner, indicating that "The changing of the culture, and that in America, people don't have too much time devoted to the marriage role and they're always pushing for time." Similarly, Bee stated that people have to return to work by Monday otherwise they would be fired, so the ceremonies must be done within a limited time frame.

Lack of Knowledge of the Rituals

Lack of ritual knowledge was another factor that the participants felt was related to the Hmong changing their traditional ritual practices. The Hmong's traditional marriage ceremony is a complex ritual where many of the Hmong traditional marriage ceremony go-betweens or *mejkoob* took years to learn the rules, proverbs, and marriage songs. Although some of the Hmong who are still in Laos may not know all the details and intricacies of the traditional marriage ceremony rituals, most of them were well-versed in the rules governing this institution. The 0.5-generation Hmong and the younger Hmong generations are not as knowledgeable about the traditional marriage ceremony rituals due to the lack of usage and participation. Neng stated that the younger generations do not know the rituals as well as do the older generations:

> Not a lot of the go-between, they don't know the rituals
> or the marriage songs any more and so they just bypass
> it or skip it. Because they don't know a certain marriage
> song or ritual then they say we'll take the penalty and
> drink to bypass it. It has been accepted by both families
> in this case to accept it.

Xue and Toua stated that due to the change in environment from
Laos to the U.S., "the traditional marriage ceremony is too
complicated for the young generation that born in the U.S. [to
learn, retain, and practice]."

Religion

Religion is another factor that has caused changes in the
traditional Hmong marriage ceremonies. Many Hmong have
converted to Christianity since their arrival in the U.S. in 1975.
In their conversion to Christianity, they have modified the
traditional Hmong marriage ceremony rituals or have abandoned
them all together and adopted the Christian traditions of marriage.
Bee shared how he modified his marriage ceremony to
accommodate the influence of Christianity:

> We did a simple one at the house. We did both, one
> traditional with the umbrella, but because my in-laws
> are Christian and their relatives are not, their relatives
> listened to my in-laws to follow the way of the Christian.
> My father-in-law lived away from his relatives, but since
> their relatives were traditional, we got some of the
> individuals from that town and planned to follow the
> traditional way. But we did not do them. I did not even
> kneel because my father-in-law did not feel that I should
> do it. My parents had a pastor to have us take our vows
> in the home [of the bride]. We also did a ceremony with
> the county for our license and a reception at our church.

We did not dress in a white gown or anything but we held a reception.

Chong stated, "The growing Hmong population that belongs to a church will affect in great deal the old practices." Religious preferences will continue to play a vital role in the type of marriage ceremony that is being practiced by the Hmong.

Significance of Hmong Rituals

Cheng stated that in Laos, the marriage ceremonies were times of entertainment for villagers and clan members. Not only were the marriage songs and proverbs entertaining for the marriage participants, but also for the spectators at the event. They also sang traditional songs amongst the official marriage party members from both sides of the families along with any villagers or clan members throughout the nights of the marriage celebration (Bla Neng Vang, personal communication, March 20, 2008). In the U.S., only a few individuals actually participate and observe marriage ceremonies, especially from the groom's side of the family. Although large numbers of people will gather for the marriage ceremony celebration, they do not understand the meaning of the rituals. Cheng spoke about the need to know the significance of the rituals to maintain its practice:

> But once in this country, the ritual has lost its meaning because people don't understand its significance any more. People don't understand what the *mejkoob* say any more. Very few people understand. The young people view it as insignificant. We need to streamline for the young people to understand the meaning. One reason why the young people lost interest is because participant don't get to participate. Only the *mejkoob* and 3 to 4 people from the groom's and the bride's side get to talk. The audience they come to watch for awhile but they lose interest and so they go home. So if Hmong

want to make it meaningful then they have to get people to make it meaningful and shortened it. I saw how rituals are done. It's a way of telling the couple about the history of the world, how they connect and relate to each other, and how they resolve problems. Nowadays it's because people come to watch for awhile and then they are bore and they lose the significance of the ritual ties of the two clans. We don't understand the rituals. The marriage ceremony rituals now, they don't sing a lot of the marriage songs anyway. Some of the *mejkoob* don't even know the songs. In a way, if you don't know the chant and the songs, it's boring. Back then, it's the songs that make marriage ceremony interesting, now it's all about the *txheej cawv* [rounds of drink] so it's boring. Now, they just quickly go through the rituals with alcohol. One way to make it meaningful for the bride and groom is to explain the rituals from the beginning so they have an understanding of the process and the importance of the situation. If they don't understand then they only know the significance of what they do but no explanation. We need to get the ladies involved in the ceremony. Some men are boring and not creative. We need to involve the women and make it interesting and streamline it to make it meaningful so that it's emotional.

Involvement of official members of the marriage party and other vital individuals, such as the bride and the bride's family, would allow active participation and bring meaning during the course of the ceremony.

Assimilation and Acculturation in the U.S.

Assimilation and acculturation to the American culture was another factor that has impacted many changes to the traditional Hmong wedding rituals. Maly stated, "Just like the

rest of the country, we, Hmong, is going away from traditions."
Many of the lengthy rituals are shortened to accommodate today's
society. Nhia indicated:

> I haven't seen a whole lot seriously, but compared now
> to the way of the past, it's shorter than the past. We kept
> every element except not as lengthy. By listening to
> parents about how long it takes back then, I guess maybe
> here too but it varies case by case but most case it's
> shorter. We are becoming more Americanized and we
> can still do shorter but have the same effect, not 3 days
> and but about 1 day ½.

Bee stated, "Another is that a lot of Hmong adopted the American
way of life. Like my uncle who knows a lot about the marriage
rituals but he doesn't follow all the steps." Nhia shared the
information about her Americanized marriage ceremony:

> We didn't do an American wedding, we just went
> downtown. We already had a community wedding the
> Hmong way. You have to fill out a form which has
> everything, your education, your parents, and then they
> verify everything to make sure that it's true. Then you
> go talk to a clergy and then a small ceremony where you
> said your I do's. It's important to make sure that it's
> legal in the American eyes.

Assimilation and acculturation are playing important roles in
shaping the Hmong marriage ceremonies in this country. It
appears that the more assimilated the Hmong become, the less
they practice their traditional marriage ceremony rituals. Meng
shared his thoughts about the future marriages as assimilation
and acculturation continue in this country:

> I speak for myself, in the future, if the youngsters have
> good job then they could do it however way that they
> want because a marriage ceremony costs about $30-
> $40,000. The traditional way of *pe* [kneel] or money

doesn't matter any more. If they have money then they give us money, but if not then they don't have to because the money that we spent raising them is more than the bride price already.

Education

Education also played an important part in the changes that have occurred in the traditional Hmong marriage rituals. The participants stated that as the Hmong become more educated and earn higher salaries, they tended to have both Hmong and American weddings. Youa agreed, "Most of the educated would have the traditional marriage but also have another nice American wedding . . . there are two ceremonies." They are more receptive to change and modify the traditional Hmong marriage rituals to emulate the mainstream culture.

Mixed Race Marriages

With the growing number of mixed race marriages within the Hmong community, changes to the traditional marriage ceremonies are inevitable. Alternative marriage ceremonies are being used and accepted by many of the Hmong parents in these types of cases. Bee stated that "Things are changing. I see that if a Hmong marries Hmong then there are high expectations on rituals, but if that person marries other ethnicities then you just let it go." It is proving difficult to have another individual of a differing ethnic group yield to the traditional Hmong marriage customs.

Money Required for Rituals

Money is yet another factor that has influenced changes

to the traditional Hmong marriage ceremony rituals. Some Hmong are not willing to pay the high costs associated with a marriage and subsequent celebration. Maly noted that:

> I think it's the lack of money and respect. Everyone works hard to earn their living and if it will save them $7,000 to $20,000, they will avoid it. There's too much freedom and too many laws protecting everything and everyone. Those that don't have a traditional marriage want the easy way out.

Some of the interviewees stated that they would not require the bride price or other payments since the cost of rasing their daughters outweighed that of the bride price. Maly noted that "Some families don't even collect money any more" when a couple marries.

Language

Most of the young Hmong in this country have some difficulty in speaking and understanding the Hmong language, and it would be difficult for them to replicate the marriage rituals of which they have limited comprehension. Even the 0.5-generation Hmong are having some challenges in speaking technical Hmong terminologies and phrases.

Collectivism to Individualistic Thinking

The last factor that has resulted in changes to the traditional Hmong marriage ceremonies is the apparent shift in thinking from a traditional collective decision-making system to one that is more individualistic. With this shift in thinking, it has resulted in many changes to the traditional marriage ceremony rituals, which mirror the mainstream mind set. Bee expanded on this notion: "Another factor is that no matter if the parents allowed or not, they will eventually live together anyway . . . if denied the marriage, the children may just run away then you can't do much, or just marry elsewhere."

Meng acknowledged the change in thinking of the younger generation:

> It depends, especially the kids who we called, *miv nyuas laib* [young Hmong who are gang related or who share little interest in the traditional Hmong culture], they don't care whether we approve or not, they live together anyway without marriage. In our Hmong culture you must have a marriage even without money they will work to pay later but must have a marriage ceremony. I know of a case where the groom wanted to pay the dowry but the girl didn't let him and so they ran away.

Based on the factors that these interviewees discussed and acknowledged, the traditional Hmong marriage ceremony rituals have been greatly affected by their resettlement and living in the U.S. With such a paradigm shift in thinking among the younger Hmong generations, it is quite possible that the Hmong marriage ceremony rituals may never be the same again as they were in their homeland. Toua concluded:

> Since we are living in this country now, acquiring some of the good ceremony rituals from this society and add it to our traditional marriage ceremony might not be bad ideas and hopefully will bridge the two societies which we are currently being caught in between. This will ensure that we preserve some [of the traditions] and give [up] on other unnecessary [ones] as we move forward and adjusting to the new environment [of this country].

Future Marriage Rituals and Ceremonies

This 0.5-generation Hmong appear to be more flexible with their children's options for a marriage ceremony. They stated that they were born and raised practicing the traditional Hmong marriage ceremony rituals, but they have already lost a great deal of their traditional culture while living in the U.S. They felt that it would be difficult to confine their children's marriage ceremony within the traditional Hmong marriage practices. About half of the interviewees stated that they would like to have both an American wedding and a traditional Hmong marriage ceremony with some modifications for their children. Cheng shared his thoughts on this notion:

> I probably like to see them have a combination wedding with church and traditional. I would like to cut the traditional Hmong marriage ceremony short. Well, streamline it so that it's short. I think that I would like to streamline it from the introduction with a couple of relatives do blessing and give advice, most important in the wedding, and then do the acquaintance following the family gathering together. And then that's it. I mean it make sense.

Maly shared her thoughts on what she would like to see in her children's marriage ceremony:

> I would like to have it done both ways, I, myself had two weddings, a Hmong one and an American one. I guess it would depend on whom he marries too. These days, there are interracial marriages and having a Hmong marriage may not be in the interest of the other family. I don't have anything against interracial marriages, but this is how I see the future.

Youa agreed that she would like to see some changes, too, for her children's marriage ceremonies:

> If they have money then I'm open to my children having an American wedding. But if they don't have money then I am okay with them just having a Hmong wedding. But I would really like to see one or two of my children

have a nice American wedding. I wish to see them have
or experience that happiness. I really wish that I had the
opportunity where I've met someone who truly love me
and that since we will only marry once, let's make it this
way. Both will work hard at it and I will support them.
However, I would not support having my children
spending $20-$30,000 charged to credit card. I think
that it speaks volumes about how much they love each
other.

Foua noted that, "I really like to see the combination of both.
Perhaps we need to see if we can combine the ceremonies into
one party to save money, etc." About half of the interviewees
felt that the marriage ceremony would also depend on the ethnicity
of their children's spouse-to-be. They would be flexible and
accommodate whatever marriage ceremony that would be agreed
upon by both the bride's and groom's parents. Foua discussed
her feelings on her daughter's future marriage ceremony:

> I go with either Hmong or American because right now,
> our children, they don't like to date Hmong any more,
> our daughter, she likes to date Hispanic and American.
> Those are the only ones she dates so we may end up
> going with whatever ethnicity she marries. I would like
> for them to follow the Hmong marriage ceremony.

Neng shared his thoughts about the uncertainty of his children's
future Hmong traditional marriage ceremony:

> Because we don't really know the rituals, we might do
> the marriage traditionally too but more the American way
> because when my children grow up, I don't know the
> rituals. I may have a traditional marriage just to get it
> out of the way but also have an American wedding also.
> It really depends on who they marry. It's not like back
> in Laos where we can control who they marry.

Even though the future generations may not have the knowledge and understanding of the traditional Hmong way of marrying, most of the interviewees shared that they would like the marrying couple to ask their parent' permission for the marriage or at the very least inform their parents of the impending marriage. Tong felt that respecting and honoring the parents of the couple is important in a marriage:

> Even if they don't want to have a traditional marriage, for the girls, they should know our culture because the groom is not Hmong. Because we are Hmong, they must respect us as parents. They must know to come to the girl's home and let the parent know about the marriage. They should let the parents know first before they start living together. Bride price, it really depends on you as mothers. When it comes to the Hmong culture of asking the parent's permission for the marriage is one thing, but when it comes to the bride price, I side with the American way. I would like to see contributions from both sides of the parents on the marriage. In this country, I don't necessary see a marriage as all about the money.

Similarly, Bee agreed that:

> I would like to have my children come to the house and make their commitment to me. I think that we just need to have both parents come together to talk about it. I don't really want an all night ritual with the *mejkoob*.

Some interviewees stated that they wanted to diverge from the Hmong traditional marriage ceremony rituals all together. Meng stated how he would move forward with his children's marriage ceremonies:

> For my children, I don't want to follow Hmong traditional marriage arrangements. If the couple has money then

after they come to ask for the marriage, we could just go to a restaurant and celebrate with just a small gathering. It doesn't have to be big. Maybe 10-20 families and not the 40-100 families.

The interviewees seemed to be passionate about the changes that have occurred in the traditional Hmong marriage ceremony rituals as they shared their hopes and wishes for their children's future marriage ceremonies. There was a wide spectrum of responses regarding the modifications and changes to the traditional Hmong marriage ceremonies as these interviewees' children marry.

Future Hmong Marriage Ceremonies

With such modifications and changes to the traditional marriage ceremony rituals among the 0.5-generation Hmong over the past 30 years while living in the U.S., the impact on marriage ceremonies for the future generation may even be greater. It is possible that many Hmong marriage ceremonies will be further simplified, retaining only the most basic elements of the rituals to appease and legitimatize for their elders. Many of the marriage ceremonies will more likely be Americanized weddings. Eventually, the Hmong will no doubt cease practicing their traditional marriage ceremony rituals and follow the mainstream American manner of marrying. Nhia described how she would try to maintain the rituals for her children:

> I feel that, the Hmong, we will lose our culture and religion eventually because our generation is the last generation to keep it and the younger they're so Americanized that they really don't care as much about their culture as we do and the older generation, and I feel that it's my job to help her understand her roots and culture, especially when I married outside of my race. I

made it so much more important to really find out about
whom I am and where I came from.

Youa believed that the rituals would eventually be lost:
In the long run we will be like the mainstream American
where we'll lose our lineage and connections. The second
generations will continue to practice some of the
traditional rituals because they watch their parents and
grandparents performing the rituals and interacting with
clans and cousins. The 3rd generations will probably
not practice any more.

Although there were some of the interviewees who feared
that the Hmong will eventually lose their traditional marriage
ceremony practices, several of them were hopeful and felt that
some of the Hmong would continue to practice their traditional
rituals if they were written down for posterity. Perhaps, there
may be some of the Hmong who will continue to maintain the
traditional rituals through taking classes and lessons from their
elders. Tong stated:
I think that no matter what, there will still be some that
will still know the Hmong rituals. So, no matter what,
the Hmong ritual needs to be done first and then if they
want to do it the American way then they can afterwards.
Because we are Hmong, we must do the Hmong rituals
first and then American. Yes, the American way is easy,
but if a girl is going to start her life, she must do some
Hmong rituals before she leaves her parents' door to start
a life with the outside. That's how I see it. Since we
don't know the Hmong rituals and so we don't have much
to comment. Had we know more, we would have a lot
to say. This speaks volume about the need to learn about
our culture and rituals.

Bee concurred that: "I think that our rituals will change. Abandon it totally, I don't think in our life time. Maybe in the next 50 years. The younger generations are learning it now. It's going away but not any time soon."

Chong stated that, "It is unavoidable that we are losing what our ancestors have left for us. Soon we will read about it only. I believed since our ancestors left China we've lost something." Cheng stated that through streamlining and simplifying the rituals, it would provide insightful meanings for the marrying couple and the participants at the marriage ceremony. It would also entice interest for the younger generations to continue practicing and maintaining the Hmong's traditional marriage ceremony rituals.

Summary

The 0.5-generation Hmong were born and raised in the traditional Hmong way of life. They are the generation who can oscillate between the traditional customs of the older generation and the more modernized younger generations of this country. They are the first generation to make significant changes to the traditional Hmong marriage ceremony rituals by modifying and simplifying these rituals to accommodate the culture demands of their exposure to the U.S. environment. As a result, some of the participants in this research study have limited knowledge of the traditional Hmong rituals and practices and will most likely soon lose the traditional Hmong practices of marriages.

After living in the U.S. for the past 30 years due to the resettlement process, there are multiple factors that have affected and influenced the Hmong's traditional marriage ceremony rituals and practices. The participants in this research project noted that changes in the traditional Hmong marriage ceremony rituals will continue to evolve and undergo further change with each subsequent generation as the length of time living in the U.S. lengthens. There were significant modifications and changes in the practice of the traditional rituals within the 0.5-generation Hmong marriage ceremonies as they married in the early 1980s to the late 1990s, and even greater changes will no doubt occur in future marriage ceremonies. As the acculturation and assimilation processes for the Hmong become more apparent, the less traditional Hmong marriage ceremony rituals will be practiced and eventually the Hmong will cease practicing their traditional rituals and become even more Americanized.

There was a wide variety of responses regarding the interviewees' knowledge of the traditional Hmong marriage ceremony rituals. A little less than half of them knew some of the traditional marriage ceremony rituals, but not all of them. While a few knew one or two of the rituals, only 5 of the 12 interviewees had knowledge of most of the traditional marriage rituals.

The responses of the interviewees' thoughts and feelings about the traditional Hmong marriage ceremony rituals were also varied. Some felt that there is a need to sustain and retain the traditional marriage rituals as they played a vital role in connecting families and clans. Others thought that eventually the traditional Hmong rituals would no longer be practiced as the Hmong would begin adopting the American way of marrying. Some of the interviewees stated that they did not like the traditional Hmong marriage ceremony rituals since the practice caused conflicts within the Hmong communities, while others felt that the need to preserve the traditional Hmong marriage ceremony rituals was important, as it defined the Hmong as a people and culture.

Some of the themes that were identified by the interviewees regarding the factors that have resulted in changes to the traditional Hmong marriage ceremony rituals were: (a) time required for marriage rituals, (b) lack of knowledge related to rituals, (c) religion, (d) meaning of rituals, (e) assimilation and acculturation to the American culture, (f) mixed race marriages, (g) money required for rituals, (h) language, and (i) the shift in thinking from collectivism to individualism. These factors have impacted some of the Hmong to consider different and varied marriage ceremony approaches upon marrying.

The majority of the interviewees believed that they would be flexible and could accommodate their children's preferences for their own marriage ceremonies. Some of them stated that the variables to determine the type of marriage ceremony for their own children would be determined by the ethnicity make-up of their children's husband or wife, religious preference, and the consensus agreement between the in-laws of the couple.

The interviewees felt that the future generations of Hmong would be reluctant to practice the traditional Hmong marriage ceremony rituals since so many of these rituals would no doubt be lost through the generations. Although there may be some Hmong who will continue to learn and maintain these traditions, most of the younger generations do not know the rituals. Eventually, the Hmong will cease to embrace the traditional rituals in marriage ceremonies and adopt the more mainstream American customs for marrying.

Chapter 5

DISCUSSION

The contents of this chapter consist of several sections that detail insights gained from this study. The focus of the first half of this chapter explores the impact on traditional Hmong marriage ceremonies as a result of the data that emerged from this study and the knowledge that was gained by the researcher. Another focus in this chapter is the application of this study in the field of organization development. The second half of this chapter details the challenges and limitations of this study along with some recommendations for further research on this topic.

The culture of a group of people is similar to that of an organism, changing, reshaping, altering, shifting, adapting to whatever environment they encounter as they evolve. It is inevitable that the Hmong are also experiencing some growth, development, and change as they continue their evolving journey from one location to the next through different countries and continents around the world. Along their journey, the Hmong began to adapt and change some of their cultural practices to accommodate the cultures of those societies in which they were living. However, regardless of the country or continent in which they resided, the Hmong tended to continue to maintain important elements of their distinctive cultural practices. Within the Hmong culture, there is a unique institution related to the marriage ceremony, which has also been changing from one generation to another and from one country to another, as the Hmong have moved and adapted to the host country's marriage ceremonies. Based on this evolution of change, the connection between organization development (OD) and this research project is that of organization culture and change. Even though the Hmong's marriage institution is changing rapidly at the individual, organizational, and systemwide levels, they have not yet abandoned it completely, as they continue to practice the basic ritual elements of a traditional Hmong marriage ceremony in most of their marriage ceremonies in the United States.

Insights From the Literature Review

This research study coincided with much of Schein's (2005) discussion on subcultures' change within a culture and also with Beckhard and Harris's (1977) open-system theory in which an organization can oscillate from one organization to another. Based on the results from this study, there were multiple oscillations of moving into and out of each other within the Hmong culture and subcultures of traditional Hmong marriage ceremonies, personal marriage arrangement preferences, and the mainstream culture and its subcultures (see Figure 1). Perhaps it was the openness of the Hmong culture to promote growth and development coupled with matching a new environment that also was opened to and supportive of further progress that the Hmong have made such perceived radical changes within a short span of time of living in the United States (Lawrence & Lorsch, 1969).

The literature review provided some fundamental background information to assist in understanding the importance of the Hmong and their traditional marriage ceremony rituals and practices. It certainly illuminated the researcher's knowledge of some of the most intricate practices and beliefs of the Hmong's customs and rituals. The researcher gained a great deal of knowledge regarding the Hmong based on their beliefs in the circle of life, the important balance between the physical world and spiritual realm, the age-old art of healing illnesses, thesophisticated and dynamic social relationship systems, the unique customs and practices of marriage ceremony rituals, the ancient religious beliefs of Animism and Ancestral Worship, and the never-ending stories of their journey from one region to another in the world in their search for the freedom to live their democratic way of life in peaceful solidarity.

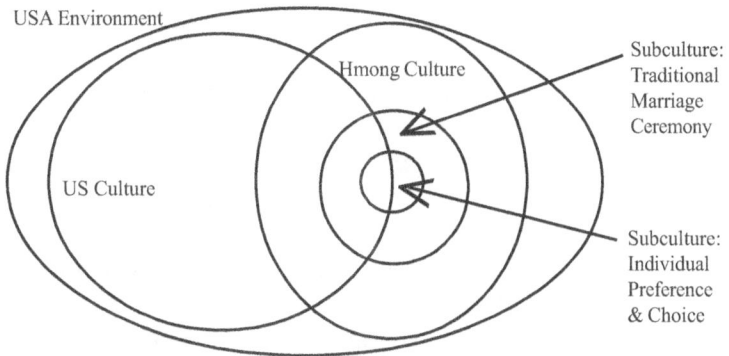

Figure 1. Open system of organization culture and subcultures of the Hmong.

Insights From the Results

Although there have been several studies that have been conducted to explore the different aspects of the traditional Hmong marriage ceremonies, this study was specifically focused on identifying some of the factors that resulted in changes in the traditional Hmong marriage ceremony ritual practices in the United States among the 0.5-generation Hmong. This study proposed to identify and learn more about these factors that have impacted the Hmong and required them to adapt and make changes to their once deeply rooted marriage rituals and practices since they have now been living in the U.S. for the past 30 years.

The themes that emerged from this research project have captured some of the factors that have precipitated the 0.5-generation Hmong to change and adapt their marriage ceremony practices to those of the mainstream American society. Although the level of assimilation and acculturation varies greatly among the 0.5-generation, most of them still believe that the traditional Hmong way of marriage is important and has relevance for the marrying couple, as they begin their life together. In a sense, the rituals in a Hmong marriage ceremony provide venues for relatives, friends, and family members to bless the marrying couple and to offer them suggestions for a successful marriage. Because of their importance in a marriage ceremony, the traditional Hmong marriage rituals will continue to play an integral part of Hmong marriage ceremonies for this generation and the next several generations that follow.

Among the 0.5-generation Hmong marriage ceremonies, there are a number of modifications and accommodations being made to the traditional marriage ceremony rituals to adapt to the U.S. marriage traditions. Some of the Hmong are still holding on to their traditional practices and rituals since they provide a strong tie and bond for the marrying individuals; however, many of them are adapting to the American way of marrying by incorporating church ceremonies along with traditional Hmong ones. Some Hmong have chosen to practice only the essential ritual elements to fulfill the traditional demands of a marriage ceremony in accordance with their families' wishes. The 0.5-generation Hmong are the generation who were raised and trained next to the older generation on the traditional Hmong marriage ceremonies, and yet they have already left behind some of the traditional marriage ceremony rituals after having been in the U.S. for what is a relatively short period of time. If this pattern continues, it is likely that the future generations would be even less apt to practice and have knowledge of traditional marriage rituals.

It is anticipated that the future Hmong generations' marriage ceremonies may vary greatly from what is being practiced today. The lack of ceremonial ritual knowledge and the changing religious practices among the Hmong from their traditional religion to Christianity are considered to be prominent factors in the reasons why the Hmong are slowly ceasing the practice of traditional marriage rituals.

It is with high hope that the unique intricacies of the traditional Hmong marriage ceremonies and rituals will continue to be documented and passed through the generations so they can be retained within the culture. By having more information on the Hmong marriage ceremonies and rituals, there will be more ways to incorporate the traditional marriage ceremonies to also reflect and accommodate the culture of the U.S. by the Hmong who are living in this country. Perhaps the younger generations will find connections to having contemporary Hmong traditional marriage ceremonies where the rituals are interwoven into an Americanized wedding to preserve the fundamental Hmong marriage ceremony elements.

The researcher was surprised to find that none of the interviewees mentioned the resistance to changing the traditional Hmong marriage ceremony to reflect the mainstream marriage rituals. Based on Beckhard and Harris's (1977) open-systems theory between two organizations and Schein's (1985) discussion on organizational culture, the 0.5-generation Hmong incorporated the two theories in conjunction with Newman and Nollen's (1998) concept on the need for organizations to make radical changes in their new environments in order to survive and advance forward in their new home in America. Perhaps the resistance to change was not an issue since they could resort to the overall Hmong culture if they should not be successful in incorporating the Hmong and American marriage ceremonies as mentioned by Schein (1985). A divergent insight on this notion may be that as the Hmong migrated from one location to another, they had to adapt and assimilate meanwhile holding fast to their traditional cultures to maintain peace with those cultures; therefore, residing in the United States and adapting to this culture was another means of survival.

Application to the Field of Organization Development

Based on the evolution of organization change, the connection between organization development (OD) and this study is organizational culture and change. Cummings and

Worley (2005) stated that when making changes to organizations, considerations need to be made about "fundamentally altering the organizational assumptions [of an organization] . . . and how it related to the environment. Changing these assumptions entails significant shifts in corporate philosophy and values and in the numerous structures and organizational arrangements that shape members' behaviors" (p. 480). The broad field of OD encompasses diverse organizations and cultures. Being culturally sensitive to organizational cultures, norms, beliefs, practices, and assumptions is vital to prevent infringing on cultural practices that may stagnate the process of change in an organization. As OD consultants work with the diverse community at large, this study would provide them with a cultural understanding of and more insight when trying to accommodate diverse cultures.

Additionally, this study would provide OD consultants with new cultural perspectives on immigrants who have recently resettled in the United States from other parts of the world. This study brings an important insight on cultural change particularly for OD consultants who work in the San Joaquin Valley of California since there have been continual waves of newly arrived refugees and immigrants who have chosen to resettle in this area. OD consultants would be able to utilize some of the results of this study to discover the factors that impact individuals or cultures to either progress or stagnate when faced with change.

Furthermore, through the process of conducting this study, the researcher was enlightened by two particular learnings. One of them was related to the field of OD. As an OD professional, the application of this cultural change study illustrated the need to be sensitive to different organizational cultures and their norms, practices, beliefs, and assumptions. Having an understanding of an organization's history and the events that have occurred over time in shaping and creating the organization's present culture is vital to assisting an organization move forward through any change processes that may be needed for growth and future development. Another insight from this study was understanding the importance of having a point of reference for using theories and models. After utilizing various OD theories and models of change to examine the Hmong's cultural changes, the researcher realized the versatility of using OD theories and models of change to frame and assess organizations from powerful and multiple perspectives.

This research study has been completed as planned and the researcher's goals have been realized. The interviewees' responses to the interview questionnaires were themed upon completion and grouped accordingly in order to draw conclusions related to the proposed research question. The interviewing process was extensive, and a great deal of time was spent in conducting the in-depth, face-to-face and telephone interviews. The researcher needed to observe the traditional Hmong protocols and etiquette when interviewing the participants by establishing rapport and trust with each of the interviewees prior to conducting the actual interview of them. With the establishment of mutual respect and trust, the interviewees were cooperative, honest, and open to sharing their marriage ceremony experiences and thoughts about the Hmong marriage ceremonies and rituals. After the interviews were conducted and transcribed, the interviewees' responses were analyzed to obtain thematic results and draw conclusions.

Limitations

There were several limitations to this study. One limitation was the lack of research and related literature that was available on the Hmong's history and culture, particularly on the focused topic of traditional marriage ceremony rituals. Because of this limitation, a great deal of the information on the Hmong's traditional marriage ceremony rituals was based on primary interviews and personal accounts of the elder marriage go-betweens and individuals in the Hmong community who had the knowledge and experience with these traditions.

Another limitation of this study was that the researcher is also a Hmong. Being a Hmong could result in some advantages of knowing some intricate information about the Hmong; however, it could pose some biases in the study, as boundaries may have been difficult to maintain throughout the process of this project. Taylor and Bogdan (1984) suggested, "Probably the best check on the researcher's bias is critical self-reflections" (p. 142). To prevent tainting the purity of the data and information obtained, the researcher had to continually use self-reflection journaling or "observer's comments" throughout this study "as a check" to maintain the process (p. 142). In addition, the researcher had colleagues read drafts and dialogued on the results to assess for the credibility of the researcher's analysis. Additionally, there were some challenges in arranging suitable times to conduct the interviews with the participants, especially with those from out of the area and state.

Finally, the last limitation of this study is that although the participants represented different states and regions in California, they all had spent a great deal of time in the Fresno County area prior to moving out of town. Therefore, the data gathered from the participants were all primarily from one area in California and cannot be further generalized unless additional studies are conducted in other states.

Future Research

Due to the limited time that was available for this research project, the participants who were chosen were readily available and were from the states of California and Utah. It would be interesting to have a broader sample of participants from other areas and states, which could be conducted with similar interviews and procedures in many of the other existing Hmong communities throughout the U.S.

Another suggestion for research would be to survey the different Hmong generations, such as the veterans, silent, baby boomer, millennial, and Y groups, utilizing a similar format and procedures from this study to gather a wider spectrum of data. A comparison and contrast study between these generations would bring about a greater understanding of the changes that have occurred in the Hmong marriage ceremony rituals since resettlement in the U.S.

To gain broader knowledge and more information about the traditional marriage ceremony and the resulting changes among the Hmong, a study could also be conducted with the Hmong throughout the various resettlement countries outside of the U.S., utilizing both qualitative and quantitative methodologies. Additionally, a quantitative study could be conducted to learn more about the actual rituals that are still currently being used by the Hmong in the U.S. and other countries to compare the various levels of change that have resulted due to the resettlement process.

Final Thoughts

After interviewing the 0.5-generation Hmong participants, the researcher sensed that perhaps there is a need to further open the lines of communication among the Hmong in order to streamline the traditional Hmong marriage ceremony rituals while still maintain some original practices, since it appears that the factors for the continuing changes in adapting and accommodating the Hmong culture to the U.S. culture are inevitable and will continue to evolve. The traditional marriage ceremony is but one among many of the traditional rituals and customs that uniquely define the Hmong. Regardless of where their journey may take them, they will continue to take their traditional cultural practices with them. They are proud of their unique history and traditional way of life. Their complex marriage ceremonies and rituals are central to the heart of what is meant to be a Hmong.

There may be some Hmong who have chosen to abandon their traditional ways of marrying by dismissing them as obsolete and irrelevant in today's climate, but there are still many of the Hmong who will continue to preserve and champion the use of the traditional Hmong rituals that have been a historical definition of who they are since ancient times. The evolution of their lives in a new country will continue to be shaped and formed by the Hmong's traditional rituals and the traditions of their new environments, but the researcher hopes that the Hmong will not allow their cultural practices to disappear completely. The Hmong have not lost their roots over the centuries of their many migrations from one location to another; they probably will not lose their roots as they strive to progress and succeed in the U.S., especially with the supportive environment based on the strength of the rich cultural diversity, strong collective belief of freedom, democracy, and the opportunity to pursue happiness.

EPILOGUE

Upon completing this study, I feel that I have gained a greater depth and understanding about the Hmong and about myself. My quest to gain greater knowledge of the intricacies of the ancient Hmong traditional marriage ceremonies and the curiosity to better understand how the Hmong have managed to maintain and preserve their traditional practices in the various societies and environments over the centuries have been realized through this study. The insights gained are multifaceted from a personal standpoint to the Hmong community and the environment that Hmong exist within a large context.

This research project has reconnected me to my roots and history at a more intimate level than before. Although we adhered to the traditional Hmong marriage rituals when my husband and I married, I really did not understand the rationales revolving the rituals. Now, reflecting on those rituals, I have a greater level of appreciation and was content that both my husband and my families decided to follow the rituals as closely to the traditional marriage in Laos as possible because I could conceptualize the changing marriage rituals with the younger Hmong generations. Additionally, the rituals involved a sense of honor, respect, humility, the sacred union of two people, and the ultimate responsibility of being accountable individuals in a committed marriage. Furthermore, I am humbled by our historical roots and evolutional journeys, as well as having tremendous respect for our strive to defend, protect, and practice our traditional customs, especially marriage rituals. Through having extensive conversations with my parents and the elders in the Hmong community, along with discovering insightful meanings as a result of this study, I am most grateful and appreciative of my parents' and our ancestors' efforts for preserving, maintaining, and continuing to teach our traditional customs from one generation to another so that my generation and future Hmong generations can thrive in the wonders of our unique and beautiful culture.

Although we have slight differences in our traditional Hmong practices, I have learned that essentially we are one Hmong. Our traditional rituals are uniquely our own. No other culture in the world practices and adheres to marriage rituals like the Hmong.

To be Hmong and have the opportunity to dwell and experience our rich traditions from the inside out is an amazaing feeling. I am hopeful that the future generations will continue to embrace the fundamental elements of this wonderful tradition. Although complex in nature, it embeds essential values that are pertinent to the coming together of oneness by two people and their families and the responsibility of being accountable individuals in a marriage.

Relative to living in this new environment where integrity, courage, knowledge, ability, and the unwilling determination to not give up thrust individuals into leadership roles, prominent positions, and making outstanding contributions to our community and the community at large, gender is slowly becoming a secondary requirement. Hmong women are beginning to undertake major positions and roles within their households, the communities, and the world of work and are gaining support for their efforts. Although traditional ritual-specific roles and practices will continue to be performed for years and perhaps even centuries to come, for now, Hmong women are gaining momentum, as their efforts and roles are beginning to be recognized and respected in the Hmong community. I am grateful and fortunate to be able to ride the waves of opportunity within the Hmong community and in this great society of America. Only in America, could I have big dreams and be given the opportunity to realize them like nowhere else in the world, regardless of my gender or heritage.

REFERENCES

Anders, L. B. (1999). Three wise men, a sacred space where
the big house stands: An introduction to storytell.
Hews & Views—A Publication of NTL Institute, 6, 1-4.
Barney, G. L. (1981). The Hmong of northern Laos. In
Glimpses of Hmong history and culture (Indochinese
Refugee Education Guides, General Information Series
No. 16, pp. 18-45). Arlington, VA: National
Indochinese Clearing House.
Beckhard, B., & Harris, R. T. (1977). *Organizational
transitions: Managing complex change.* Menlo Park,
CA:Addison-Wesley.
Berg, B. L. (2007). *Qualitative research methods for the
social science.* Boston, MA: Pearson Educational.
Bertrais, Y. (1978). *The traditional marriage among the
white Hmong of Thailand and Laos.* Chiang Mai,
Thailand: Hmong Center.
Bliatout, B. T. (1982). *Hmong sudden unexpected nocturnal
death syndrome: A cultural study.* Portland, OR:
Sparkle.
Bliatout, B. T. (1986). Guidelines for mental health
professionals to help Hmong clients seek traditional
healing treatment. In A. S. Deinart, B. T. Downing,
& G. L. Hendricks (Eds.), *The Hmong in transition*
(pp. 349-363). New York: Center for Migration
Studies of New York and The Southeast Asian Refugee
Studies of the University of Minnesota.
Bonner, B., & Chang, Y. (1995, April 16). Hmong families:
A world apart. *Saint Paul Pioneer Press*, 9A.
Bridges, W. (2003). *Managing transitions: Making the most
change.* Cambridge, MA: Da Capo Press.
Cappelletty, G. G. (1986). *Factors affecting psychological
distress within the Hmong refugee community.*
Unpublished doctoral dissertation, California School
of Professional Psychology, Fresno.

Cerhan, J. U. (1990). The Hmong in the United States: An overview for mental health professionals. *Journal of Counseling and Development, 69*, 88-92.

Cheon-Klessing, Y. C., Camilleri, D. D., McElmurry, B. J., & Ohlson, V. M. (1988). Folk medicine in the health practice of Hmong refugees. *Western Journal of Nursing Research, 10*, 647-660.

Community Planning Organization, Inc. (1980). *The Hmong in St. Paul: A culture in transition.* St. Paul, MN: Author.

Conquergood, D., Thao, P., & Thao, S. (1989). *I am a shaman: A Hmong life story with ethnographic commentary* (Southeast Asian Refugee Studies Occasional Paper No. 8). Minneapolis: University of Minnesota, Center for Urban and Regional Affairs.

Cooper R. (1988). *Vanishing cultures of the world: The Hmong, a guide to traditional lifestyles.* Singapore: Times Editions Private Limited.

Countries of the world: And their leaders yearbook. (1990). Farmington, MI: Gale Research.

Creswell, J. W. (2002). *Research design: Qualitative, quantitative, and mixed methods approaches.* Thousand Oaks, CA: Sage.

Culas, C. (2004). Innovation and tradition in rituals and cosmology: Hmong messianism and shamanism in southeast Asia. In N. Tapp, J. Michaud, C. Culas, & G. Y. Lee (Eds.), *Hmong/Miao in Asia* (pp. 97-126). Chiang Mai,Thailand: Silkworm Books.

Cummings, T. G., & Worley, C. G. (2005). *Organization development and change.* Mason, OH: Thomson South-Western.

Dana, A. F. (1993). Courtship and marriage traditions of the Hmong (Master's thesis, California State University, Fresno, 1993). *ProQuest Information and Learning Company.* (UMI No. 1355382)

Dao, Y. (1982). Why did the Hmong leave Laos? In B. T. Downing & D. P. Olney (Eds.), *The Hmong in the West, observation and reports* (pp. 3-18). Minneapolis, MN: Center for Urban and Regional Affairs.

Dao, Y. (1993). *The Hmong at the turning point.*
Minneapolis, MN: WorldBridge Associates.

Downing, B. (1986). Language and literacy. In G. L.
Hendricks, B. T. Downing, & A. S. Deinard (Eds.),
The Hmong in transition (pp. 213-216). New York:
Center for Migration Studies of New York.

Egan, M. T. (2002). Organization development: An
examination of definitions and dependent variables.
Organization Development Journal, 20(2), 59-69.

Faller, H. S. (1985). Parental needs of immigrant Hmong
women: Surveys of women and health care providers.
Public Health Reports, 100, 341-343.

Fendya, J. A. (1995). Being a Hmong in America: A
phenomenological study of female Hmong college
students (Doctoral dissertation, California School of
Professional Psychology, 1995). *Dissertation Abstracts
International, 56*(10-B), 5883.

Fink, J. (1981). Clan leadership in the Hmong community of
Providence, Rhode Island. In B. T. Downing & D. P.
Olney (Eds.), *The Hmong in the West, observation and
reports* (pp. 21-27). Minneapolis, MN: Center for
urban and Regional Affairs.

Fong, R. (2004a). Contexts and environments for culturally
competent practice. In R. Fong (Ed.), *Culturally
competent practice with immigrant and refugee children
and families* (pp. 39-59). New York: The Guilford
Press.

Fong, R. (2004b). Overview of immigrant and refugee
children and families. In R. Fong (Ed.), *Culturally
competent practice with immigrant and refugee children
and families* (pp. 1-18). New York: The Guilford
Press.

Forsyth, D. R. (2006). *Group dynamics.* Belmont, CA:
Thomson Learning.

Freeman, A. M. (1996). The values and legacy of the
founders of NTS: An interview with Ken Benne. *Journal
of Applied Behavioral Science, 32,* 332-344.

Geography Department. (1996). Laos in pictures. In M. M.
   Rodgers (Ed.), *Visual geography series* (pp. 7-18,
   38-44). Minneapolis, MN: Lerner.
Gonen, A. (1993). *The encyclopedia of the peoples of the
   world.* New York: Holt.
Goodstein, L., & Burke, W. (1995). *Creating successful
   organization change. Organizational dynamics:
   Managing organizational change* (Special Report).
   New York: American Management Association.
Hamilton-Merritt, J. (1993). *Tragic mountains—Hmongs, the
   Americans, and the secret wars for Laos, 1942-1992.*
   Bloomington: Indiana University Press.
Hardy, R. J. (1992). *Government in America.* Boston:
   Houghton Mifflin.
Hayes, C. L. (1987). Two words in conflict: The elderly
   Hmong in the United States. In D. E. Gelfand &
   C. M. Barresi (Eds.), *Ethnic dimension of aging*
   (pp. 79-95). New York: Springer.
Hmong Youth Cultural Awareness Project. (1994). *A free
   people: Our stories, our voices, our dreams.*
   Minneapolis, MN: Author.
Hoang, G. N., & Erickson, R. V. (1982). Guidelines for
   providing medical care to Southeast Asian refugees.
   Journal of the American Medical Association, 248,
   710-714.
Hockings, P. (1993). *Encyclopedia of world cultures.*
   Boston: Hall.
Johnson, C., & Yang, S. (1992). *Myth, legends and folk
   tales from the Hmong of Laos.* St. Paul, MN:
   Macalester College.
Keown-Bomar, J. (2004). *Kinship networks among Hmong-
   American refugees.* New York: LF Scholarly.
Koumarn, Y. S. (1978). The Hmongs of Laos. In *Glimpses of
   Hmong history and culture* (Indochinese Refugee
   Education Guides, General Information Series No. 16,
   pp. 3-4). Arlington, VA: National Indochinese
   Clearing House, Center for Applied Linguistics.
Kunstadter, P. (2004). Hmong marriage patterns in Thailand
   in relation to social change. In N. Tapp, J. Michaud,

C. Culas, & G. Y. Lee (Eds.), *Hmong/Miao in Asia*
(pp. 375-420). Chiang Mai, Thailand: Silkworm Books.
Lao, T. (2008). *The quotations page*. Retrieved October 27,
2008, from http;//www.quotationpage.com/quote/24004
Lee, G. Y. (1982). *Contemporary Laos: Studies in the
politics and society of the Lao people's democratic
republic*. New York: St. Martin's Press.
Lee, G. Y. (1996). *Cultural identity in post-modern
society: Reflections of what is Hmong?* Retrieved
December 19, 2007, from http://www.garyyalee.com
Lee, G. Y. (2005a). *Cultural identity in post-modern
society: Reflections on what is Hmong?* Retrieved
December 19, 2007, from http://www.garyyialee.com
Lee, G. Y. (2005b). *Current Hmong issues: 12-point
statement*. Retrieved December 19, 2007, from
http://www.garyyialee.com
Lee, G. Y. (2005c). *Household and marriage in a Thai
highland society*. Retrieved December 19, 2007, from
http://www.garyyialee.com
Lee, G. Y. (2005d). *The religious presentation of social
relationships: Hmong world view and social structure*.
Retrieved December 19, 2007, from http://www.
garyyialee.com
Lee, G. Y. (2005e). The shaping of traditions: Agriculture
and Hmong society. *Hmong Studies Journal, 6*, 1-33.
Retrieved March 23, 2008, from http://ww.garyyialee.com
Lee, G. Y., & Tapp, N. (2007). *Current Hmong issues: 12-
point statement*. Retrieved December 19,2007, from
http://www.garyyialee.com
Lemoine, J. (1986). Shamanism in the context of Hmong
resettlement. In A. S. Deinard, B. T. Downing, &
G. L. Hendricks (Eds.), *The Hmong in transition*
(pp. 337-348). New York: Center for Migration Studies
of New York and The Southeast Asian Refugee Studies
of the University of Minnesota.
Lemoine, J. (2005). *What is the actual number of the Hmong
in the world?* Retrieved December 19, 2007, from
http://www.hmongstudies.org/HmongStudiesJournal

Lewin, K. (1951). *Field theory in social science.* New York: Harper & Row.

Lewis, E., & Lewis, P. (1984). *People of the golden triangle.* New York: Thames & Hudson.

Lie-Yong, G., Yang, P., Rai, K., & Vang, Y. P. (2004). Hmong children and families. In R. Fong (Ed.), *Culturally competent practice with immigrant and refugee children and families* (pp. 122-145). New York: Guilford Press.

Lin, K, Inui, T. S., Kleinman, A. M., & Womack, W. M. (1982). Sociocultural determinants of the help-seeking behavior of patients with mental illness. *The Journal of Nervous and Mental Disease, 170*(2), 75-85.

Lo, F. T. (2001). *The promised land: Socioeconomic reality of the Hmong people in urban America (1976-2000).* Bristol, IN: Wyndham Hall Press.

Manio, E. B., & Hall, R. R. (1987). Asian family traditions and their influence in transcultural health care delivery. *Children's Health Care, 15*, 172-177.

Martin, J. (2002). *Organization culture.* Newbury, CA: Sage.

McInnis, K. (1991). Ethnic-sensitive work with Hmong refugee children. *Child Welfare, 70*, 571-580.

Meredith, W. H., & Rowe, G. P. (1986a). Change in Lao Hmong marital attitudes after immigrating to the United States. *Journal of Comparative Family Studies, 17*, 117-126.

Meredith, W. H., & Rowe, G. P. (1986b). Change in Hmong refugee marital attitudes in America. In A. S. Deinard, B. T. Downing, & G. L. Hendricks (Eds.), *The Hmong in transition* (pp. 121-133). New York: Center for Migration Studies of New York and The Southeast Asian Refugee Studies of the University of Minnesota.

Meyers, C. (1992). Hmong children and their families: Consideration of cultural influences in assessment. *The American Journal of Occupational Therapy, 46*, 737-744.

Mickey, M. P. (1981). The Hmong: Dying of culture shock. *Science, 212*, 1008.

Morgan, G. (1997). *Images of organization*. Thousand Oaks, CA: Sage.

Moua, T. 2003). *The Hmong culture: Kinship, marriage, and family systems* (Master's thesis, University of Wisconsin-South, 2003). Retrieved February 20, 2008, from http://www.wstout.edu/lib/thesis/2003/2003/mouat.pdf

Moua, T. (2006). Change and choice: Hmongs' identification with a homeland (Doctoral dissertation, Alliant International University, 2006). *ProQuest Information and Learning Company*. (UMI 3251223)

Mouanoutoua, V. L. (1989). *Validity and reliability of the Beck depression inventory adapted Hmong version*. Unpublished master's thesis, California State University, Fresno.

Mua, N. K. (2002). *Hmong marriage in America—The paradigm shift for a healthy generation*. Bangkok, Thailand: Prachoomthong Printing Group.

Newman, K. L., & Nollen, S. D. (1998). *Managing radical organizational change*. Thousand Oaks, CA: Sage.

Ng, F. (1995). *The Asian American encyclopedia*. New York: Marshall Cavendish.

Nishio, D., & Bilmes, M. (1987). Psychotherapy with Southeast Asian American clients. *Professional Psychology Research and Practice, 18*, 342-346.

Organization Development Institute. (2001). *The international organization development code of ethics*. Retrieved January 8, 2001, from http://members.aol.com/odinst/ethics.html

Organization Development Network. (2001). *ODN mission, vision, values, responsibilities*. Retrieved January 20, 2005, from http://www.odnetwork.org/visionmissionvalues.html

Pfaff, T. (1995). *Hmong in America: Journey from a secret war*. Eau Claire, WI: Chippewa Valley Museum Press.

Pfeifer, MN. E., 7 Lee, S. (2000). *Hmong population, demographic, socioeconomic, and educational trends in the 2000 census.* Retrieved March 22, 2008, from http:// hmongstudies.com/ 2000HmongCensus Publication.pdf

Pfeifer, M. E., & Yang, K. (2000). *Profile of Hmong education attainment.* Retrieved March 22, 2008, from http://hmongstudies.com/ 2000HmongCensusPublication.pdf

Quang, V. D. (2004). The Hmong and forest management in northern Vietnam's mountainous areas. In N. Tapp, J. Michaud, C. Culas, & G. Y. Lee (Eds.), *Hmong/Miao in Asia* (pp. 321-331). Chiang Mai, Thailand: Silkworm Books.

Quincy, K. (1988). *Hmong: History of a people.* Spokane, WA: Eastern Washington University Press.

Robbins, C. (1987). *The ravens.* New York: Crown.

Ruona, W. E. A. (2005). Analyzing qualitative data. In R. A. Swanson & E. F. Holt (Eds.), *Research in organizations: Foundations and methods of inquiry* (pp. 233-264). San Francisco: Berrett-Koehler.

Schanche, D. A. (1970). *Mister pop.* New York: Mckay.

Schein, E. (1985). *Organizational culture and leadership: A dynamic view.* San Francisco: Jossey-Bass.

Schein, E. (2005). Taking organization culture seriously. In W. J. Rothwell & R. L. Sullivan (Eds.), *Practicing organization development* (pp. 365-375). San Francisco: Pfeiffer.

Schein, E. H. (1999). *Process consultation revisited: Building the helping relationship.* Reading, MA: Addison-Wesley.

Strauss, W., & Howe, N. (1991). *Generations: The history of America's future, 1584 to 2069.* New York: Morrow.

Symonds, P. V. (2004). *Gender and the cycle of life calling in the soul in a Hmong village.* Seattle, WA: University of Washington Press.

Tannenbaum, R., & Hanna, R. (1985). *Holding on, letting go and moving on: Understanding a neglected perspective on change. Human systems development.* New York: Wiley.

Tatman, A. W. (2004). Hmong history, culture, and
    acculturation: Implications for counseling the Hmong.
    Journal of Multicultural Counseling and Development,
    32, 222-233.
Taylor, J. S., & Bogdan, R. (1984). *Introduction to*
    qualitative research methods: The search for meanings.
    New York: Wiley.
Taylor, J. S., Bogdan, R. C., & Walker, P. (2000).
    Qualitative research. In A. E. Kazdin (Ed.),
    Encyclopedia of psychology (pp. 489-491). New York:
    Oxford University Press.
Thao, X. (1986). Hmong perception of illness and
    traditional ways of healing. In A. S. Deinard, B. T.
    Downing, & G. L. Hendricks (Eds.), *The Hmong in*
    transition (pp. 365-378). New York: Center for
    Migration Studies of New York and The Southeast Asian
    Refugee Studies of the University of Minnesota.
Uba, L. (1992). Cultural barriers to health care for
    Southeast Asian refugees. *DHHS PHS, Public Health*
    Reports No. 107, 544-548.
U.S. Census Bureau. (2008). *United States census 2000.*
    Retrieved February 20, 2008, from http://www.census.gov
Vang, C. Y. (2008). *The people of Minnesota: Hmong in*
    Minnesota. St. Paul: Minnesota Historical Society Press.
Vang, L., & Lewis, J. (1990). *Grandmother's path*
    grandfather's way. Rancho Cordova, CA: Authors.
Westermeyer, J. H., Neider, J., & Callies, A. (1989).
    Psychosocial adjustment of Hmong refugees during their
    first decade in the United States. *The Journal of*
    Nervous and Mental Disease, 177, 132-139.
Yang, K. (1997). *Hmong men's adaptation to life in the*
    United States. Retrieved December 20, 2007, from
    http://www.hmongstudies.org/HmongStudiesJournal
Zemke, R., Raines, C., & Filipczak, B. (2000). *Generations*
    at work: Managing the clash of veterans, boomers, Xers,
    and nexters in your workplace. New York: American
    Management Association.

APPENDIX A

RITUAL STEPS OF A TRADITIONAL HMONG

MARRIAGE CEREMONY RITUAL
Ritual Steps of a Traditional Hmong
Marriage Ceremony Ritual

The following are the sequential ritual steps of a traditional Green Hmong marriage ceremony rituals on both sides of the bride's and groom's families.

Essential Sequential Steps Taken on Groom's Side

Before the Marriage Ceremony Day at the Groom's Home

1. *Lwm qab ntawm qhov rooj/nqee plig*: a chicken ceremony at the front door of the groom's home to welcome the bride's soul into the groom's household and the ancestors or lineage of the groom.
   Significance: The Hmong believe that when a woman marries a man, her spirit belongs to her husband's family, and the family needs to welcome her soul into their home by performing a ritual at the door of the groom's home. This ritual is performed by a member of the groom's family, preferably an aunt with a live chicken in hand, making a circle above the bride's head as she walks into the groom's home for the first time. After this ceremony, the bride is considered the groom's wife, even though the formal marriage ceremony has not yet been performed. The bride cannot enter anyone else's home other than the groom's for the next 3 days. If the bride should walk into any other homes, a penalty of money may be forced on the bride and the groom.
   2. *Moog thoob xu*: the process of letting the bride's parents know that the bride and groom have agreed to marry each other.

Significance: Two male individuals from the groom's side take some cigarettes and money to the bride's home to let her parents know the bride's whereabouts and the bride/groom's agreement to a marriage. Sometimes, this was traditionally the time to set up a date for the marriage ceremony rituals at the bride's home.

3. *Thov Mejkoob*: finding the marriage go-between or the representative of the groom's parents.

Significance: This is the process of finding a marriage go-between to represent the groom's side of the family during the marriage ceremony ritual. This person speaks on behalf of the groom's family to the bride's marriage go-between person and spearheads the entire marriage ceremony on behalf of the groom's family. The Hmong are a modest group of people with strong emphasis on proper standard code of conduct and etiquettes on traditional rituals. It would be considered ill mannered, rude, disrespectful, and arrogant for either parents to negotiate openly about their children's marriage arrangements without having a marriage go-between. Without a marriage go-between, the marriage proposal would sometimes be considered a hoax.

4. *Moog saib nam txiv*: 3 days after the bride and groom have eloped, they normally return to the bride's home to visit her parents.

Significance: Traditionally, an individual may not have many outfits and so after 3 days, the groom has to take the bride to her home to visit her family and obtain some change of clothes.

Day of Marriage Ceremony (About Noon)

5. *Tsaa Qhua Sawv Kev*: a formal ritual process before the groom's official marriage party leaves to the bride's home for the marriage ceremony.

Significance: The groom's side of the family begins their part of the marriage ceremony at the groom's home. A sequential ritual is performed followed by a feast with the groom's relatives and friends prior to leaving to the bride's home. This feast calls for the groom's relatives to bless and wish the groom's official marriage party with good luck and a safe return. The groom's official marriage party consists of the following individuals:

   a. *Vauv* (groom): carries the blanket to the bride's home. Upon returning from the bride's home, the groom carries the bride's belongings and another individual would carry the blanket.

   b. *Bride* (nyaab): the bride

   c. *Mejkoob* (marriage go-between): the marriage go-between representative of the parents (depending on the dialect of the bride; if the bride is Green Hmong then there is only one marriage go-between, but if she is White Hmong then there are two marriage go-betweens). The marriage go-between spearheads the marriage rituals on behalf of the groom's family throughout the marriage ceremony.

   d. *Nam txais tsuab or nam ua luag* (bride's maid): A single, never been married individual from the groom's family must accompany the bride at all times throughout the marriage ceremony at the bride's home. Depending on the type of marriage arrangement, a special name is given to the bride's maid during the marriage ceremony. The bride's maid is called *nam txais tsuab* if the groom asks for the bride's hand in marriage (*nqeg tsev has*). The name *nam ua luag* is given to the bride's maid when the marriage arrangement is either elopement, bride capture marriage, or any other types of marriage arrangements. The rule governing who would quality to be a bride's maid is that the individual has to be single and never been married before and be of the same generation or of younger generation than that of the groom. It is considered improper and disrespectful to have an

older generation be the bride's maid even though it
would be appropriate to have a younger generation
individual take this role. The Hmong place high value
on generation of individuals and their status within
their community; that is why it is important to
follow this rule during the marriage ceremony process.

e. *Pij laaj* (groom's kneeling partner): This person
has to be a single male from the groom's side and
accompanies the groom when kneeling or *pe*. This
person is a younger generation individual who helps
the older generation groom relative kneel. It is
uncustomary to have the older generation be a
pij laaj to help kneel with the younger generation
groom.

f. *Tug Ris Nraa* (the Marriage Lunch Basket Carrier):
This person has to be a single male from the
groom's side and carries the Marriage Lunch Basket
to and from the bride's home.

6. *Noj sus tom ntog kev*: lunch or the meal between the
parents' homes.

Significance: It is customary that a meal is eaten half
way to and from the bride's home. Before eating the meal, the
mejkoob has to make food offerings to the spirit of the area for
blessing and a safe passage or journey to the bride's home.

The Day of the Marriage Ceremony at the Bride's Home

1. *Noj nam txiv pluag mov ua ntej has tshoob:* the
bride's parents' feast prior to proceeding with the marriage
ceremony rituals.

Significance: It is customary for the bride's parents to
prepare a feast awaiting the groom's official party. Upon their
arrival, the meal is eaten prior to proceding with the marriage
ceremony rituals.

2. *Lub rooj has tshoob*: the official marriage ceremony table.

Significance: The marriage go-betweens use this table to negotiate the bride price, *choj tshoob* or marriage bridge, *qhwv hauv caug* or permission for the younger sister to marry if the older sister has not married yet, *npluas* or wrong doings or penalties for any wrong doings, and any other marriage discussion items.

Official Marriage Participants: The following are the official marriage participants from both sides of the families, who sit around the marriage table and actively participate throughout the marriage rituals, with the exception of the Marriage Lunch Basket carrier, bride, and the bride's maid. All participants are male, even though there are females in name, a male representative or her husband would sit in her place:

    a. *vauv*: groom

    b. *mejkoob*: marriage go-between from groom's side

    c. *mejkoob*: marriage go-between from bride's side

    d. *pij laaj*: best man

    e. *nam dlaab txiv dlaab*: bride's uncle and aunt from mother's side

    f. *pug laug yawm laug*: bride's father's older brother and wife

    g. *nam ntxawv txiv ntxawv*: bride's father's younger brother and wife

    h. *puj nyaaj hab txiv kwj*: bride's aunt and uncle from her father's side (this is more prominent with White Hmong than Green Hmong)

    i. *nam laug txiv laug*: bride's older married sister and brother-in-law

    j. *nug tij*: bride's older brother

The following individuals do not sit around the marriage table but play an important role throughout the marriage ceremony rituals.

    a. *kaav xwm* (master of ceremony): This person

regulates the marriage ceremony rituals from the beginning to the end of the marriage celebration.

b. *tub lau cawv* (alcohol servers): two alcohol servers, one on each side of the marriage table. Their primary role is to serve alcohol every time proposal are agreed upon and a round of drinks is established.

c. *tshwj kaab* (the chef or main person who prepares dishes for the meals): spearheads preparation of food, especially main dishes for the multiple feasts and meals throughout the marriage ceremony.

d. *nam ua mov* (rice cooker): responsible for ensuring that there is sufficient cooked rice and other dishes for the multiple meals throughout the ceremony.

3. After all the negotiations have been completed and the marriage celebration begins, the following rituals are done sequentially throughout the marriage ceremony with the official members of the marriage parties from both sides. (Note that the proceeding rituals are only some of the central rituals and most often are done in an elopement type of marriage arrangement.) Keep in mind that the rounds of drinks always begin at the front end of the table and then go to the back end of the table. One round of drinks means that the individuals at the front end of the marriage table begin the drinks and everyone on both sides of the table must drink the exact drinks sequentially until the last individuals finish the same drinks before a new round of drinks can begin. Each round of drinks has a meaning and is labeled as the following:

Significance. The following rounds of drinks signify an agreement on that particular item or discussion item before a new item is proposed. These rounds of drinks are similar to conditions of a contract for which individuals who drank them testify to the couple's marriage commitment to each other. The indicated rounds of drinks are some of the more common proposal and agreements made during a marriage ceremony. The round of drinks depends on the type of marriage arrangement and the bride's parents' decision.

    a. *Cawv xwm* (the check-in drink): a small bowl of alcohol along with one small cup of alcohol and one small cup of tea. All members of the marriage ceremony must drink this before they take their seats at the marriage table.

    b. *Cawv txais qhua* (greeting the guest drink): This round of drinks is a welcome and greet drink for all the participants at the marriage table.

    c. *Cawv qhe roog* (the official drink to open the marriage ceremony rituals): This round of drinks marks the beginning of the marriage ceremony drinks at the marriage table.

    d. *Cawv dlaws khaus* (the take-off-of-the-shoe drink): The literal translation for this round of drinks is for the individuals to take off their shoes inside of the bride's home during this ritual; however, in actuality, this is the drink to decide the pair of alcohol cups that the two sides of the official parties are willing to agree on to drink throughout the ceremony ritual. Meaning, if the bride's side drinks two small cups of alcohol during each round of drinks, then the groom's side would have to drink four small cups. The small cups of drinks double that of the bride's side for the groom's.

    e. *Cawv txhib qhua ce rooj* (the checking of the participant to sit around the marriage table): There is no drink involved in this ritual.

    f. *Cawv poob plaag* (recognition of the bride's family and relatives): The groom and the *pij laaj* kneel two times each for all the bride's family and extended family members who are the official bride's marriage party.

    g. *Cawv suav yaig* (drink to check omen according to

boiled chicken): Each person sitting around the table gets a boiled chicken to check for good luck according to the chicken that they are given. Normally, each person has to check the boiled chicken's feet, tongue, and skull for omen. If the omen indicates negative then the person who checked that chicken must drink a couple of alcohol cups to right the wrong.

h. *Cawv ntau dlaab tshoob* (offerings to the marriage spirit): Because the Hmong believe in spirits, each member of the table has a spoon of rice and stands around the marriage table while the *mejkoob* sings a special marriage song to the Marriage Spirit. Everyone has to be actively listening to the song since they all have to use the spoon in hand to make a clockwise circle every time the *mejkoob* finishes a verse.

i. *Cawv paam thaaj tshaab thaaj* (acknowledgment drink of the bride's family and relatives): The groom and his best man kneel twice to all of the bride's relatives. After this, the bride's side will have the bride's brothers stand next to the groom and best man to drink a big cup of alcohol in acceptence of acknowledgements.

j. *Cawv sus* (the lunch drink): This drink signifies that lunch or a meal will be served for the people sitting around the table immediately following this round of drinks.

k. *Cawv theem tsum* (the postponed or break drink): This round of drinks is agreed upon to give the individuals sitting   around the marriage table a break prior to resuming the rituals.

After this drink, the groom's *mejkoob* can ask the bride's *mejkoob* to continue the rituals without postponing the rituals if they want to proceed quickly through the rituals. Upon resuming the rituals, the *mejkoob* on the groom's side will go back to his party's side and vice versa for the bride's side. The drinks will start from the reverse end of the table, which is the inside of the house to the outside of the house.

l.   *Cawv tshais* (the breakfast drink): Although no food is actually being   eaten for breakfast, the idea and recognition of having breakfast is being acknowledged through this round of drinks.

m.   *Cawv kaw moo* (the gift, conclusion of the marriage ceremony, and acquaintance drink): This is the drink for the bride's elder brother to share the gift and money that are given to the bride and groom to begin their life together. After the gifts and money are given to the groom's *mejkoob*, he sings a marriage song to the bride's parents and relatives to thank them for the gifts.

After this last round of drinks, the bride's relatives introduce (*zeem vauv*) themselves to the groom. Each acquaintance is two drinks for the groom and two for the particular relative who is introducing himself or herself to the groom. At this point, the groom's *mejkoob* will sing a special marriage song to ask the bride's *mejkoob* for the Marriage Umbrella.

n.   *Cawv sawv kev* (the departure drink): This drink signifies that the bride and groom's party are getting ready to leave the bride's home.

o.   *Cawv fuam cum* (the last drink): This drink is to conclude the marriage rituals at the marriage table.

After this drink, the groom looks for the bride's parents to thank them and respectfully bids farewell to them by kneeling two times to each parent.

4. *Taij Kau Tshoob*: The groom's marriage go-between asks for the return of the Marriage Umbrella from the bride's marriage go-between prior to departing from the bride's home.

Significance: Because of the importance of the Marriage Umbrella, the groom's marriage go-between must sing a special marriage song for the return of it before the groom's official party can depart from the bride's home. This step is done after the *Cawv kaw moo*.

5. *Qab faib sav*: the separation of life and soul chicken.

Significance: when the bride and groom and all of the groom's marriage party have exited the bride's home, the groom's *mejkoob* will tear a cooked boiled chicken in half, leaving the half without the head to the bride's mother and taking the half with the chicken's head for the bride. This is symbolic as it separates the life of a daughter and a mother. It signifies that mother and daughter now live separate lives with equal balance of life and spirit.

Day After Marriage Ceremony When Bride/Groom Return Home

1. *Nub tub nyaab rov lug tsev*: the day the official groom's party is returning home from the bride's home after the marriage ceremony.

Significance: On the day that the groom's official marriage party is returning home, the groom's parents would have already informed all of the groom's relatives to gather at the groom's home to celebrate and welcome the party back. The groom's family and relatives have been celebrating with food and wine while they waited for the marriage party to return home. Upon the marriage party's arrival at the groom's home, two elders would greet the *mejkoob* at the door with eight small alcohol cups. As they welcome the marriage party the *mejkoob* will drink four cups and the two elders will drink four cups of the alcohol. After this small ritual, the members of the marriage party are permitted to enter the groom's home and are officially welcomed back home.

2. *Tam mejkoob and nkaw cov lug coj lug*: thanking the *mejkoob* and bidding the marriage message from the bride's family to the groom's family; blessing of the newly wedded couple ceremony.

Significance: The groom's family thanks the official marriage party individuals for their support and willingness to participate in the marriage ceremony. Official marriage party members are thanked separately, and the male relatives who attend the ceremony would kneel twice to thank them. Each member also receives a small amount of money and a small pork rib portion for the help in the marriage ceremony.

This ceremony ritual also allows the *mejkoob* to share the marriage ceremony experience at the bride's home along with the gifts and blessings that the bride's parents and relatives have given to the newly wedded couple to begin their life together. The *mejkoob* also blesses the couple and wishes them a long life filled with good fortune, health, happiness, and many children. This is an opportunity for elders and relatives to bless the couple with many good wishes.

Essential Sequential Steps Taken on Bride's Side

The traditional rituals prior to and after the marriage ceremony occur similarly as the groom's side. These rituals happen concurrently at the groom's and the bride's home, with the exception of the *Day of the Marriage Ceremony at the Bride's Home*. On the day of the marriage ceremony, both sides of the families come together to negotiate and celebrate at the bride's home.

Before Marriage Ceremony Day

1. *Thaum luag tuaj thoob xu*: Informants at the bride's home to let the parents know the elopement (marriage) of their daughter and the groom.

Significance: Two male elders from the groom's family would go to the bride's home to inform the bride's parents that the groom and their daughter have chosen to marry and have already eloped to the groom's home. At this time, the bride's parents will call an elder male relative, called *Txiv Tsawb Tshoob*, to be the representative or spokes person for the bride's parents and go-between during this process.

Txiv tsawb tshoob: This person represents the bride's parents in the *thoob xu* process and sets up a date for the marriage ceremony. This individual may not necessarily be the same person as the *mejkoob* since the role is different.

Significance: Due to the modesty of the culture and the etiquettes of a marriage, this person is asked to speak on behalf of the bride's parents prior to having a marriage go-between person, because the marriage ceremony has not officially begun.

2. *Thov mejkoob*: the process of selecting a marriage go-between to speak on behalf of the bride's parents.

Significance: The bride's side of the family also has a marriage go-between during the negotiation process of the marriage. This person speaks on behalf of the bride's parents throughout the marriage negotiation process at the bride's home.

Day of Marriage Ceremony

1. *Nub ntxhais vauv tuaj ua tshoob*: the arrival of the groom's official party at the bride's home.

Significance: The marriage ceremony day begins with the arrival of the bride and groom or the groom's official party. Prior to the bride and groom's arrival, the bride's parents will have slaughtered a pig to prepare a special feast to thank the bride's official marriage party in advance for participating in the marriage ceremony. While they await the arrival of the groom's official party, the family will have called all of the bride's relatives to dine and share in this special feast.

2. *Tug kaav xwm lug nqug lub rooj has tshoob*: The master of ceremony sets the marriage ceremony table to begin the marriage negotiation process.

Significance: The *mejkoob* from both sides of the families sit around this table as they negotiate marriage items. The bride and her family, along with her relatives, normally sit in a different room and away from the groom's party and the marriage table. The bride's family does not sit around the marriage table. The individuals sitting around this table at this time are the two *mejkoob* or marriage go-betweens, as they negotiate and agree on marriage discussion items. The groom's family is customarily responsible for most of the marriage celebration expenses.

3. *Txheeb lub kawm su*: checking the items in the groom's official marriage party's Marriage Lunch Basket.

Significance: The *Kaav xwm* check the Marriage Lunch Basket to ensure that all the contents are there, especially the four feet of the two chickens. The chickens are eaten during the meal between the families; however, the feet are significant and therefore are saved. The chicken feet are particularly important as they are the omen of the couple's life together. If all of the necessary contents in the Marriage Lunch Basket are not there, the *Kaav Xwm* or the master of ceremony for the marriage celebration will not allow the marriage ceremony to begin, and the groom's party may be penalized to drink a couple of cups of alcohol.

4. *Ntau Nco hab khoom phij cuam rua to ntxhais*: gifts and monies given to the bride. Monies are given to certain bride's relatives to ensure the success of the marriage, especially the bride as she becomes a wife to her husband. It is considered an honor to be asked as a participant in this process.

Significance: These individuals are asked to secure and oversee the marriage of the bride and groom. If there should be problems in the long run with the couple, these individuals are to be informed to counsel the couple. Each of these individuals also gives a special gift to the bride and groom, along with some money to jumpstart and anchor the beginning of the bride and groom's life together. For example, a participant may give $100 along with a valuable traditional Hmong artifact. Specifically, Hmong artifacts such as silver bars, gold chains, Hmong traditional baby carriers, traditional Hmong outfits for the bride, and so forth.

5. *Txiv cob txheeb*: the marriage ceremony accountant.

Significance: This individual keeps track of all the gifts and money given to the bride and groom. At the end of the marriage ceremony, he is responsible for declaring the monies and gifts that the bride's parents and relatives have given to the bride and groom to the groom's *mejkoob*. The list of gifts is read and accounted for in front of the groom's *mejkoob* to share with the groom's family upon returning home.

6. *Kawm Noj Sus*: the Marriage Lunch Basket.

Significance: One leg along with the tail of the pig that was slaughtered for the main marriage ceremony feast (*Tug npua luam xwm*) must be cut and be given to the groom's family on the day that the marriage ceremony concluded. There are also two cooked chickens, one male and one female, included in the Lunch Basket. If the Marriage Lunch Basket from the groom's family has two spoons then the bride's family will match it with two additional spoons for a total of four spoons, and some cooked rice on the day that the bride and groom return home.

After the Marriage Ceremony When Bride and Groom Left

1. *Tam mejkoob*: thanking the marriage go-between and the official marriage party ritual.

Significance: thanking the *mejkoob*, the *kaav xwm*, the *tshwj kaab*, and the *nam ua mov* for their help in completing the marriage ceremony ritual and celebration. Due to the elaborate and intensity of the marriage ceremony, many relatives and friends had come to help, so the bride's family use this time to thank them all for their support and help throughout the ceremony and celebration.

APPENDIX B
SYMBOLISM OF MARRIAGE ARTIFACTS

The following are artifacts for a traditional marriage ceremony rituals:

1. *Lub kaus tshoob*: The Marriage Umbrella (see Appendix G for a photograph of the Marriage Umbrella).

Symbolism: the umbrella with a *suav ceeb* is very symbolic as it contains *kev ua neej hab qhwv plig nyaj plig kub plig tub plig kib tuab si rua huv lub kaus* or the spirit of fortune, love, children, and the way of life within it. The *suav ceeb* or a black and white striped cloth about 2" in diameter and about 1 yard long must be wrapped around the umbrella in a special way. If the cloth is tied as a knot onto the umbrella, the groom and the *mejkoob* are penalized with money and have to drink a couple small cups of alcohol. As a former *mejkoob*, marriage go-between, Xay Leng Mouavangsou (personal communication, August 27, 1996) indicated that it is very important to make sure that the cloth wrapping the umbrella is not tied into a knot as it would symbolize that the groom would, in the future, not love the bride but will torment her instead. Ka Xiong (personal communication, December 31, 2007) stated that the umbrella is very symbolic since it contains within it everything that the bride was blessed with for her married life. Ka Xiong said, "*Txuj kev ua neej nyob taag nhro rua huav lub kau ua tsoob*" or the way of life is wrapped inside the marriage umbrella. Symonds (2004) similarly indicated that the umbrella holds within it all the good spirits who entered the earthly realm at the bride's birth.

Note: *Suav ceeb* is typically worn by Hmong women as a decorative piece on their headdress. The color of this umbrella must be black with a handle. The umbrella is closed with the *suav ceeb* wrapped around the bottom half of the umbrella.

2. *Pob choj*: a blanket, wrapped within it two bottles of wine, is strapped by a female headdress cloth called *hauv phuam*.

Symbolism: In Laos, the blanket is needed in case the groom's official party has to spend the night(s) at the bride's home. To show that the bride is very valuable and that the groom would stay at the bride's home for as long as it takes to have her hand in marriage, the groom's official party may spend multiple nights to complete the ceremony process. Depending on the complexity of the marriage ceremony, sometimes the marriage celebration and negotiation may take several days or even weeks to complete.

3. *Kawm su*: the Marriage Lunch Basket.

Symbolism: The Marriage Lunch Basket must contain the following items: one small package of salt, two boiled chickens, and some cooked rice. The boiled chickens would be eaten for lunch prior to entering the bride's home, and the four chicken feet must be saved as evidence. If the chicken feet are not in the Marriage Lunch Basket when the *kaav xwm* checks it, the groom's party would be penalized with two small cups of alcohol or sometimes be fined a small amount of money.

The distance from the groom's home to the bride's may be far, so a lunch basket would be packed for the marriage party to eat along the way. Even if the distance is near, it is customary to eat a meal between the homes.

4. *Npua luam xwm*: the Marriage Pig for the main marriage celebration feast.

Symbolism: the pig that the groom's family provides for the marriage celebration. This pig must measure six fists on the roundest side of the pig's belly. It is the main animal used for preparing for the main marriage celebration feast. Although the pig would be slaughtered for the feast, the bride's family must save the tail part, along with one thigh of the pig, as this uncooked portion would be packed and given to the bride/groom's party when they return home.

5. *Luam yeeb*: cigarettes.

Symbolism: In Laos, before a request or proposal is made, the *mejkoob* from the groom's side would give each male adult (on the bride's side) who came to take part in the negotiation process two pinches of cigarette leaves. However, in the USA, individuals would be given two store-bought cigarettes. This is a respectful and humble way to begin discussing a new proposal or discussion item. Cigarettes are only used during the thoob xu process and when the marriage go-between's negotiate the bride price at the early stages of the marriage ceremony rituals at the bride's home.

      6. *Cawv*: alcohol.

      Symbolism: Whenever an agreement on a proposition or request is reached, two small cups of alcohol are drank among the marriage go-betweens or the official marriage party members, as they bear testaments to the marriage proposal agreements. The Hmong have a strong belief that during the marriage ceremony all the alcohol that is being served must be in two's, which represents the groom and bride.

      7. *Nyaj txag*: money.

      Symbolism: Money is used to pay for the bride price and any penalties or wrong doings during the marriage negotiations. Sometimes, money is paid to the bride's parents to form a new tie or marriage bridge between the two clans or lineage if the present marriage is the first marriage among them. Sometimes, money is paid to a bride's older sister if she is still single and the bride marries first. Money given to the older sister is a considered a way of asking the older sister's approval for the younger sister's marriage.

APPENDIX C
INTRODUCTION TO THE PARTICIPANTS

Thank you for participating in this interview with me today. You are being asked to participate in this project to determine the Hmong marriage values. This information is being collected as a part of a study conducted by Choua Mouavangsou at the Marshall Goldsmith School of Management and Organizational Development at Alliant International University. The information will be used to determine how living in the United States has affected the 0.5-generation Hmong traditional marriage ceremonies and rituals.

Your participation in this interview is voluntary. If you choose not to be involved in this study, please tell me now. Your name will only appear on the consent form and not on any other documents. To keep your information confidential, I will assign a numeric number to your responses for identification purposes only. In addition, when I finish transcribing your responses from the audiotape, I will erase the audiotape and destroy it.

APPENDIX D
INFORMED CONSENT FORM

I agree to participate in the dissertation project, "Traditional Hmong Marriage Values and Practices: Influence and Change as a Result of Immigration," being conducted by the researcher, Choua Mouavangsou. I am aware that participating in this research will involve the following:

A. The researcher will ask questions about my opinion on Hmong marriages.

B. I can choose to have the interview audiotaped by the researcher. If I choose to have the interview audiotaped, I understand that the audiotape will be erased and destroyed after the information has been transcribed and interpreted. I also understand that the researcher will keep my informed consent form and my recorded audiotape locked in separate file cabinets in a locked room to further secure my information and confidentiality.

C. I will complete a demographic questionnaire.

I understand that my participation in this interview is voluntary and that there is neither reasonable nor foreseeable risk involved in this study. I also understand that there is no compensation or benefits for me as a participant. If I decide not to be involved in this study, I will be free to withdraw from this study at any time without penalty. I understand that my name will not appear on the demographic questionnaire and my answers will be kept strictly confidential.

Should I get sick for any reason and unable to continue in the interview process, I would be able to contact the researcher or the committee chair, Dr. Toni Knott, at the Marshall Goldsmith

School of Management and Organizational Studies at 559-253-2262. In addition, I can contact either the researcher or Dr. Knott for an executive summary of the project at the end of the study.

My signature below indicates that I am willing to participate in the interview under the conditions stated above.
Participant
Signature:_____ Date:_____

Researcher
Signature:_____ Date:_____

APPENDIX E
DEMOGRAPHIC INFORMATION

Please read each group of statements or questions below carefully and fill in the blank, mark on the line or circle the response that best describes you.

1. Please circle one:
   Male   Female
2. How old are you?
   Age:_____
3. How old were you when you came to the United States of America (USA)?
   A. What year did you come to the United States:_____
4. What grade were you when you started school in the USA?
5. What is your marital status? Please circle one:
   Single Married Divorced/Separated Widow/Widower
6. What is the highest grade or degree you have completed?
   Please circle one of the grade levels or college degrees:
   High School:
   9 10 11 12
   Years in College:
   13 14 AA/AS
   15 16 BA/BS
   17 18 MA/MS
   19 20+ PhD
   Vocational/Trade School
   1   2   3
7. Do you have any children?
   Number of children:_____
8. Do you understand and speak Hmong fluently?
   Yes   No
9. Do you understand and speak English fluently?
   Yes   No
10. What is your religion?_____

APPENDIX F
SEMISTRUCTURED INTERVIEW QUESTIONS

1. Do you know what the traditional Hmong marriage
    ceremony rituals are?

2. How do you feel about the traditional marriage ceremony
    rituals?

3. Do you think that there are **some changes** or differences
    in the Hmong marriage ceremony rituals now compared to
    the traditional marriage ceremony rituals in the past?
    a. What are some of those changes? How do you feel
        about those changes?
    b. What are some of **the factors** that cause the Hmong to
        divert from practicing traditional marriage ceremony
        rituals?
    c. How do you feel about the influence of this country
        on marriage rituals and practices?

4. How was your marriage ceremony done?
    a. What are some of the factors that would cause your
        marriage ceremony to be done that way?
    b. How would you like to see your children's marriage
        ceremonies done?

5. How do you see the future of Hmong marriage ceremony
    rituals and practices now and the future?

6. Is there anything else that you would like to add?

APPENDIX G
TRADITIONAL HMONG MARRIAGE UMBRELLA

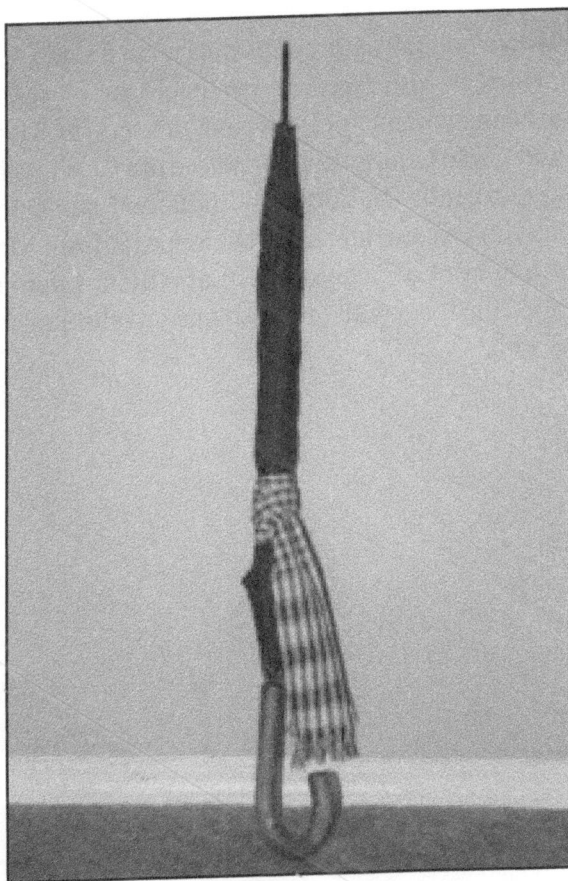

About The Author

Choua Mouavangsou is a counselor with Fresno Unified School District. She received her bachelor of science in Business Management in 1990 and masters in Marriage, Family and Child Counseling in 1996 from California State University, Fresno. In 2009, she obtained her Doctor of Psychology in Organizational Development from Marshall Goldsmith School of Management at Alliant International University. She lives with her husband and children in Central California.